D1737452

The Literary Storefront

THE LITERARY STOREFRONT
The Glory Years

Vancouver's Literary Centre 1978-1985

TREVOR CAROLAN

Foreword by Jean Barman

Mother Tongue Publishing Limited
Salt Spring Island, BC
Canada

MOTHER TONGUE PUBLISHING LIMITED
290 Fulford-Ganges Road, Salt Spring Island, B.C. V8K 2K6 Canada
www.mothertonguepublishing.com
Represented in North America by Heritage Group Distribution.

Book Design by Mark Hand
All photographs taken at the Literary Storefront unless otherwise stated. Photographs within are by Milton Bingham, Peter Haase, Literary Storefront members and unknown.
All photographs courtesy of the UBC Library, Rare Books and Special Collections, Literary Storefront fonds unless otherwise noted.

Printed and bound in Canada.

All efforts have been made to locate copyright holders of source material wherever possible.

Mother Tongue Publishing acknowledges the assistance of the Province of British Columbia through the B.C. Arts Council, and we gratefully acknowledge the support of the Canada Council for the Arts, which last year invested $157 million in writing and publishing throughout Canada. Nous remercions de son soutien le Conseil des Arts du Canada, qui a investi 157$ millions de dollars l'an dernier dans les lettres et l'édition à travers le Canada.

LIBRARY AND ARCHIVES CANADA CATALOGUING IN PUBLICATION

Carolan, Trevor, 1951-, author
     The Literary Storefront : the glory years : Vancouver's literary centre,
1978-1984 / Trevor Carolan ; foreword by Jean Barman.

Includes bibliographical references and index.
ISBN 978-1-896949-52-9 (paperback)

     1. Literary Storefront--History--20th century. 2. Canadian literature--
British Columbia--Vancouver--Societies, etc.--History--20th century.
3. Vancouver (B.C.)--Intellectual life--20th century. I. Title.

PS8005.L58355 2015   C810'.6071133   C2015-904048-5

For Rudi and Gretchen Diesvelt,
the soul of old Kitsilano

And to all the members and supporters
of the Literary Storefront,
the spirited and the forgotten,
the eclipsed and the shining

Contents

Foreword

The history of Vancouver has many parts. The Literary Storefront is one of them. In operation from 1978 to 1985, the Literary Storefront opened its doors to writers and poets and to those aspiring to become such. Its optimism encouraged numerous of our leading literary lights to hone their talents.

The Literary Storefront facilitated Vancouver's transition from then to now. A dozen years ago, I published a biography of a woman with two strikes against her in the Vancouver of then. Constance Lindsay Skinner was determined to be a writer, and she was a woman. Unwilling to give up on her dream, she realized it at the cost of leaving behind the city and province of her upbringing. Perforce living in New York City, she Americanized the names of places in her poems, short stories and adult and young people's books whose content drew on the Vancouver and British Columbia she knew and loved. Constance Lindsay Skinner's tradeoff was not unique in the Vancouver of then, but rather reflected what long existed. To be "literary" was to head elsewhere or, for the select few, almost wholly men, who were admitted into its ranks, to acquiesce to the closed world of the University of British Columbia.

Change was in the air by the time of the Literary Storefront opened in 1978. Along with some mainly juried venues for publishing poetry and prose, small presses around the province had grown over the past decade from a handful to over two dozen. More and more writers, albeit mostly publishing elsewhere, called Vancouver home.

As Trevor Carolan masterfully evokes and the many images attest, the Literary Storefront energized Vancouver's transition from then to now. There men and women gained in self-confidence, reading their work aloud and listening to that of others, coming to understand what was necessary to get published and to be recognized and, for some others, realizing their talent did not measure up to their hopes for a writing life. Founded and overseen by poet and writer Mona Fertig, the Literary Storefront was a meeting place, a coming together place that made it acceptable to be creative.

By the time the Literary Storefront shut its doors in 1984, the Vancouver of now was in view. Consequent on the Literary Storefront and also coincidental to it, the city and province were maturing. As opposed to writers and poets having to be imported from away for special events, their local and regional counterparts might be called upon. Expo 86, along with the Vancouver Centennial Commission commemorating the city's hundredth anniversary, opened up Vancouver to British Columbia, Canada and the world. I was parachuted onto the already established Commission as its sole female member, indicative of the lagging acceptance of women as writers and in general. There, to come full circle, I chaired two committees encouraging local writing and publishing not unlike the Literary Storefront, as would *BC BookWorld* and the BC Book Prizes founded shortly thereafter.

Vancouver and British Columbia are special places for many reasons, among them the Literary Storefront that not so long ago made it all right to be from here and to do great things. It was no longer necessary to live elsewhere to be a writer, a poet, someone who put words on paper in ways that gave others pleasure in their reading or their listening. The Literary Storefront gave a cohort of men and women the will to be creative in ways that echo into the present day. Entering into The Literary Storefront is to experience that transformation.

Jean Barman, Vancouver, 2015

Trevor Carolan, Joe Plaskett, Marya Fiamengo, Alvin Balkind, 1981,
Bau-Xi Gallery opening, Photograph courtesy of Canada Wide Media, *TV WEEK*

Introduction

Founded by Mona Fertig, a Vancouver poet, the Literary Storefront thrived in Vancouver from 1978 to 1985. A unique literary centre and cultural institution, it was situated in the historic Gastown area near the Pacific Coast city's inner harbour waterfront. During its heyday, the Storefront had some 500 members—poets, playwrights, novelists, readers, editors, publishers, journalists, teachers and everything in between—and during its first two years alone drew more than 13,000 people to its diverse events,[1] as well as for its lending library of 2,000 books by mainly Canadian authors. People gravitated here for individual reasons—to meet, talk and learn about writing, publishing and the world of books and literature. Some came for comradeship and open-access solidarity; many came simply to see and hear or rub shoulders with an amazing range of established literary personalities. The Literary Storefront's hundreds of public readings and workshops drew, among other notables, Margaret Atwood, Michael Ondaatje, Dorothy Livesay, Jane Rule, Al Purdy, Earle Birney, bill bissett, Audrey Thomas, Lawrence Ferlinghetti, P.K. Page, Stephen Spender, Edward Albee and Elizabeth Smart. It was a home-port reading base too for the West Coast's own growing legion of writers: Roy Kiyooka, Susan Musgrave, Keith Maillard, Carolyn Zonailo, Maxine Gadd, Peter Trower and scores of others were familiar headliners. Yet the Literary Storefront was never about simply readings, performances or any one thing. Canada had seen nothing quite like it previously, nor has it since.

This book of oral history and archival research recounts the visionary Literary Storefront project begun by Fertig—the daughter of Vancouver painter George Fertig—that was continued for a time by a collective and a pair of migrant Americans, Wayne Holder and Tom Ilves, the latter who would emerge surprisingly on the world political stage years later as the President of Estonia.

Preliminary work toward this project began with a "brief history" chapbook produced by Mona Fertig for the Reckoning '07 Conference organized by Alan Twigg at Simon Fraser University's downtown Vancouver campus. The conference focused on the past and future of British Columbia writing and publishing. Aware that the Literary Storefront's history had disappeared, Mona gave out the limited edition chapbook to various B.C. publishers and attendees during the coffee breaks. It became clear to a number of veteran British Columbia writers during this event how significantly the region's literary culture was being academized and, simultaneously, how much of that history was already being lost within this institutionalization. Elders of the West Coast's literary tribe were steadily passing away.

When Fertig published her own book about her father (*The Life and Art of George Fertig*) as the third in Mother Tongue Publishing's Unheralded Artists of BC series, it was not difficult to observe that the memory of the Literary Storefront itself was fading in the same romantic twilight. I knew a number of the artists cited in her book and saw that they too, like veteran writers associated with the 1950s and '60s, were vanishing stories. As if in confirmation, two recent feasibility studies for an ambitious and expensive Literary Arts Centre for Vancouver developed by the Association of Book Publishers of B.C. and its supporters make no reference to or recognition of the history of Vancouver's first grassroots literary centre; so, this book will serve as a necessary archival document for students of BC's literary history.

I'd had my own start as a serious writer during the heyday of the old Storefront after returning to Vancouver from several years in northern California. When I began asking old friends and colleagues about their recollections of the Literary Storefront, this led organically to inquiries among an even wider circle of writer contacts. Literally everyone I spoke with recalled the centrality of the Storefront years as a unique moment in the West Coast's literary and cultural history.

As the nature and scope of the conversation grew, the essential nature of the Literary Storefront began to assert itself again. For almost everyone, the Storefront had been more than just a stop on the path to establishing a career. It had served as a society of friends; some attended readings and workshops regularly for the conviviality and networking opportunities it offered, others were more single-minded regarding their own work and picked selectively at the cornucopia of events on a year-round basis. If, like most of those who congregated there, you didn't have a lot of money in your pockets, that was all right too; for a time, this was Vancouver's bohemian consular centre. If you wanted to know about the Zen of writing, to get your mojo working at a first open-mic reading, to engage in searching deliberations with other fledgling writers or to read their work from the shelves of books along the wall—this was the place for you.

During the run of the Literary Storefront, Vancouver was still an old-school seaport town. The World Expo of 1986 that would accelerate the demolition of heritage buildings and change the city's architectural face irrevocably had yet to happen. Downtown, the Hastings Street tenderloin, if rugged, was not the combat zone the provincial and city authorities would allow to fester there; it still housed the city's best newsagents, a variety of colourful pawnshops, Gabor the Cobbler and the landmark Only Seafood Café. Nearby, Chinatown was still thriving, and the back-alley Green Door and Red Door Restaurant and B.C. Royal Café on Pender Street were old reliables. The Ho Ho at East Pender and Columbia Street remained the city's unofficial late-hours eatery for musicians and jazzoids, and two short blocks away Vie's nine-table Chicken and Steak House at 209 Union Street still had legs until 1979, serving up what locals could relate to as soul food.

It wasn't perfect, but Vancouver was a town of possibility. Architect Arthur Erickson had earned international renown. Bill Reid was associated with the Pacific Northwest Coast's native art renaissance. Jean Coulthard was a nationally important composer, and B.C. poet Phyllis Webb was an equally respected radio broadcaster. Painter Joe Plaskett, although long a resident of Paris, still called the old capital city of New Westminster, a drive up Kingsway, home, as did novelist Sheila Watson and longtime *Perry Mason* television series star Raymond Burr. Actor Chief Dan George from the Tsleil-Waututh reserve in North Vancouver had already become a beloved elder to many Canadians, and Bruno Gerussi starred in what seemed like a never-ending hit playing a drift-log salvager in the weekly CBC-TV series *The Beachcombers*. That Jimi Hendrix's grandmother Nora had worked as a chef at Vie's Chicken and Steak place for years while living on East Georgia Street in the nearby Strathcona district, and that her guitar wizard grandson had stayed with her many times and sharpened his chops at Monday night sessions in the clubs around the corner, only added to the sense that this was a place that had known famous times, sprung some big names, that things could happen here. Among writers, Malcolm Lowry had spent the better part of fifteen years nearby, struggling with the making of his celebrated novel *Under the Volcano* and a series of cloudy follow-ups. Poet Earle Birney had established the country's first serious creative writing program out at the University of BC (UBC), and Marya Fiamengo, an ardent nationalist, had established a feminist ethic in poetry from the early 1960s onward and was outstandingly supportive of other writers.[2] English professor Warren Tallman from the same school had been instrumental in inviting writers from the American Black Mountain and beat spectrum to the city for almost two decades, as well as shepherding a group of former students into teaching and media careers of significance. Novelist Margaret Laurence and future Nobel Prize winner Alice Munro both lived and worked in the city during formative stages in their careers, while the luminous Ethel Wilson wrote for decades from her home overlooking English Bay. An active theatre community produced an impressive roster of actors and directors.

The late 1960s through to the 1980s was a time of Pierre Trudeau-era nationalist arts funding to Canadian publishers, and British Columbia had a budding regional literary and publishing scene, which included Intermedia Press, Sono Nis Press, New Star Books, Pulp Press, Talonbooks, Commcept Publishing, Orca Sound Publishing, Hancock House, Harbour Publishing, Oolichan Books, Riverrun Books, Vancouver Community Press, blewointment press,[3] as well as an emerging group of women who were starting their own writing/ literary businesses. Carolyn Zonailo writes:

> A real growth spurt in literary and publishing and printing activities was initiated by women in Vancouver. Caitlin Press was founded by myself in 1977; The Literary Storefront in 1978; Press Gang Printers & Publishers in 1975; and the literary magazine *A Room Of One's Own* was founded by a collective of women in 1975. These new literary and publishing enterprises initiated by women complimented those literary small presses and endeavours begun a few years earlier by male literati such as Very Stone House founded by Pat Lane and Seymour Mayne; Blackfish Press founded by Allan Safarik and Brian Brett, among others.[4]

In step with Vancouver's emerging non-academic growth in literary publishing was its downtown pulse. Pulp Press had an office up the street from what would become the Literary Storefront's Gastown central location; Press Gang was not far off, nor was Cobblestone Printing. Since the early 1960s, poet bill bissett had been running blewointment press "from a secret location, collating on his living room floor, or conducting contract talks from the nearest phone booth. Some of his best contracts were written on postcards, and he sought out and published many new, especially downtown, poets."[5] Downtown Eastside poet Gerry Gilbert's mimeographed *B.C. Monthly* had survived from 1972 onward.

Carolyn Zonailo and
bill bissett

Richard Pender Books, 1974,
Vancouver Archives
CVA-778-270

Vancouver remained a swinging, neon town renowned among
North American musicians for the high tenor of its talent and night-
life. The Main Street and Hastings cabaret district that sent acts like
Cheech and Chong, Bobby Taylor and the Vancouvers and others to
stardom was entering its last stand. The Lotus Hotel across the road
from the old Vancouver Sun building at Pender and Abbott remained a
favourite media watering hole, and up-and-coming writers still hoped
to meet veterans like the *Vancouver Sun*'s Allan Fotheringham, Jack
Webster and Marjorie Nichols there from time to time. Five minutes
walk away, the north end of Granville Street retained its colonial-era
atmosphere with fine tailors, upscale shoe emporia, James Inglis Reid's
grand old British butcher shop and Woodwards' $1.49 day. Free parking
in the immediate area was an inducement to downtown shoppers.

Bookshops meanwhile, new and used, flourished. Duthie's, Mac-
Leod's, Colophon, Richard Pender Books, William Hoffer, Bookseller
and the leftist outlet Spartacus were all in bloom. For bohemian die-
hards, the Classical Joint on Carrall Street was the town's perennial
evening-until-late jazz nexus. A handful of Irish pubs and run-of-the-
mill watering holes opened early for the area's large population of

single-room occupants—old loggers, fishermen, boom-men, miners and sundry veterans who'd somehow slipped through the social net. Working-class, shake and shimmy, down at heel, creative and cheap, the Gastown-Downtown Eastside district was a natural magnet for the young and artistic with a dream, and for outsiders of every social hue. It was the ideal location for a walk-in literary centre. It still is.

Novelist David Watmough reflects:

I'm eighty-seven and we're talking about thirty or more years ago, but my overall impression of Vancouver during the period of the Literary Storefront is that, until then, how lonely and isolated we were as artists and writers here . . . There was a pervasive sense of remoteness, and the atmosphere between the West and the East was quite hostile. You had the counterculture and the Peace Movements, but everything from Toronto came a week late in the mail. And literature never got quite the thrust that the visual arts did . . . We had various little power circles here—UBC, the CBC, they were sources of money . . . Even within our own literary tribe there were lots of little tribes.[6]

Poet Cathy Ford adds:

When I came from the far north as a Creative Writing student at UBC, I suffered various types of culture shock . . . there were warring factions in literary Vancouver. Literally, people who were rude to one another, gossiped loud and long about each other, and never invited one another to read at or attend readings. The academic centres were most easily identifiable for these sins . . . UBC, SFU, Capilano College, Douglas College, VCC, and the library system all overlapped one another. Meanwhile, experimental and profoundly exciting things went on downtown, in various art galleries, in Kitsilano, at bookstores and storefronts, at Western Front in combined art and literary openings, and political actions. The most challenging, progressive written work and broadside, chapbook or book publication was being done outside the formally identifiable affiliations. For someone eager to experience a sense of community, I had a lot to think about in terms of inclusiveness, personal and professional conduct, integrity.[7]

My own encounter with the Literary Storefront came by word of mouth. I was riding in a car downtown, crammed among new faces after reconnecting on the Royal City's running trails with Ron Tabak.[8] We'd been schoolmates, and he'd gone on to pop stardom as the magnetic singer with Prism, one of Vancouver's first international rock acts.

Ronnie and I ran long-distance in high school. Tall and lean, he'd always been a little faster than I was. Ronnie stuttered, but he let his hair grow long and could shake it; when he belted out a chart-busting tune like "Armageddon," all the glitches disappeared, and you knew you were listening to a real star. Ronnie lived the pop world high-life for a few years. I'd seen his posters for a huge concert in New York's Central Park when I was out on the road myself, hustling readings back east. His gold records had that sparkle dust up on the wall at his place up the road.

Now we were in a car full of Ronnie's pals, jamming out the windows. Susie Whiten, a blues singer, asked who I was. Flipping my notebook to the poems I wrote to keep myself sane in a heavy day job, I said I was a writer. Susie reached through the mob for a scan of my lines.

"You oughta get down to the Storefront and read these," she said.
"What?"

"The Literary Storefront, in Gastown. My friend Mona runs it. Go down to an open-mic session, listen to other poets, get up and read your stuff, two or three poems like these. See what people think."

One Sunday, I took Susie's advice. The first thing you noticed after you climbed the stairs in Gaslight Square at 131 Water Street was the Storefront's brickwork, funky and kind of comfy like North Beach near City Lights in San Francisco. People read in turn; there were a lot of women. I waited, listening. Nobody got put down. When I was invited up, it all went fine. People offered polite applause. At 27, it was my first public reading in town.

During a break, someone explained that it was a women's group reading—feminists and lesbians. In my newness, my enthusiasm, I'd missed all that. When I'd given my name to read, someone had simply noticed that I'd travelled some distance, and they'd been decent enough to give me a shot. When the penny dropped, I smiled at their kindness, nodded in thanks and left soon after. I would return many times.

For young writers like me, the Literary Storefront was an unofficial post-graduate education centre. It was where a generation of Vancouver writers, surfing somewhere between the nationalist and the as-yet-unformed multicultural waves in CanLit, could learn how the writing and publishing game ticked. It was a chance to become part of a community—and by the late 1970s, there was a constituency in Vancouver that needed precisely this. At the same moment, in the Smiling Buddha or any other rundown club that would have them, a similar generation of young punk rockers was figuring out the music world, and a new wave of young painters and sculptors were reimagining their creative missions in the common, low-rent environments of Gastown, Chinatown and the Downtown Eastside. Meantime downtown, the Vancouver School of Art still featured some writing-related events, readings and talks, while the Alcazar Hotel, growing seedy at the corner of Dunsmuir and Homer, was a particular favourite watering hole of the town's creative arts community. The Video Inn at 261 Powell Street hosted events as well.[9] A few blocks north brought you to the 1950s Vancouver Art Gallery on 1145 West Georgia Street where literary events such as the memorable reading by Russian poet Yevgeny Yevtushenko took place in 1974.

Against this background, in 1978 the Literary Storefront would emerge right out of the starting blocks as an incubator for the literary arts in a Pacific Coast town that had long been devoted more to hard work and real estate speculation than literature. Devoted to writers and writing, high-brow literary theory from Paris and East Coast universities never transplanted well in the Literary Storefront's earthy, practical loam. If there was intellectual debate, it was on couches during random drop-in sessions with friends or strangers met while perusing the bookshelves or the framed ephemera on the walls. More likely, it was during or after a reading or workshop presentation. The Storefront hosted literary and arts events and endured financial wobbles of every sort, not uncommon for most non-profit arts organizations. That's what made the place as likeable as it was. It was the Gastown donkey engine in the West Coast's arts scene, chugging along indomitably toward the Word, the Sound, the Beat. Ironically, that wasn't far from the mission that its founder Mona Fertig, a working-class poet and young literary organizer from Burnaby, had envisioned when she realized what she could do now that she'd grown up. Here then, is the way it was at the Literary Storefront, when in the pursuit of happiness, Mona Fertig, Vancouver's legendary unaffiliated literary force, hung out her shingle at age twenty-four and single-handedly got Vancouver's writing and literature jumping in a whole new way. It was a courageous idea and enormous accomplishment for a young woman whose life so far, while rich in art and creative inspiration, had flirted around and faced down the poverty line. Heaven only knows what so many of us in the West Coast's writing community would have done without it.

Hail to the Muse,

Trevor Carolan, Vancouver 2015

Mona Fertig, 1973, Granville Street,
Foncie's Fotos

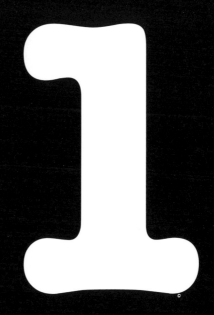

1

An Innocence Like Rolling
Thunder: Mona Fertig

Born in Vancouver in 1954, Mona Fertig spent her early childhood in the beachside Kitsilano area. Her father, George, was a painter and an outsider who endured commercial rejection throughout his career. From Alberta, he came of age in the Depression when the West saw hunger marches and riots involving strikers and the police. While working two years at the zinc smelter in Trail, B.C., he was branded a Communist for his union activities and forced to move on again. According to Joe Jankola, a local, "It didn't matter what the guy was; if you were against the system you were a Communist . . . boy, I tell you, they had the police hunting out these guys, and anybody that was involved with the union . . . It was 'get out of town or else.'"[10]

In Vancouver, George began to paint, studying evenings at the Vancouver School of Art at the old Vancouver (Central) High School at Cambie and Dunsmuir, where Fred Amess, Bert Binning and Jack Shadbolt all taught. With a passion for Jungian psychology, his work was characterized by images of the land and saltchuck—symbols of life's temporal and eternal energies, of healing and quietude in a search for transcendence. He was known as the "Moon Man."[11]

George met Evelyn Luxa, Mona's mother, at the Stanley Park teahouse after World War II. Part Ukrainian and Czech, Evelyn was a gorgeous dark-haired, olive-skinned woman. She danced well and loved movies, art and books. Evelyn worked as a receptionist and earned extra money using the skills she'd learned from her mother in reading tea leaves, cards and palms for her friends. Judith Copithorne recalls her:

[Evelyn] was an impressive person and well worth knowing, what one might call a practical mystic. She held the family together, I believe, and, so far as I could see, exuded good humour, intelligence, sociability, practicality and kindness, as well as presenting herself in beautiful and colourful garb on what must have been very little money and time. She didn't give up on someone. She loved George . . . She gave Mona a very open view of life, a wonderful ability to see much farther than most people are allowed to see in our society.[12]

Mona's dad never become a part of what Joe Plaskett described as the "cozy freemasonry" of Vancouver's painterly elect that could refer each other to paid teaching positions, commissions, appointments and back or judge each other through committees for grants and travel.[13] His work did draw a positive review by Mildred Valley Thornton in the *Vancouver Sun,* noting its "peculiar haunting beauty." George's calm, surreal paintings exuded a dreamy sensuality that even today continues to be remarkable. Was it this visionary, probing style that alarmed the status quo all along? When George died in 1983, painter LeRoy Jensen recalled:

He didn't put up with any compromise . . . You saw these other people . . . they all had these cushy jobs at the VSA and spoke of themselves as some kind of revolutionaries. They were the most conservative people you could imagine. They never took chances . . . there, on the other hand, was George. I don't even remember how he used to make money.[14]

Those encountering his daughter Mona through her Storefront years might add that the apple doesn't fall far from the tree.

At the age of ten, Mona moved with her parents and younger sister, Moana, to an older house in Burnaby on Pioneer Avenue, down from the Old Orchard shopping centre on Kingsway. She first began gathering a few friends together there in her early teens. The Fertigs didn't have a car, so Mona cleaned and transformed the garage into a clubhouse for the small outsider element she chummed with at Moscrop Secondary School down the hill. They were comfortable with the batik décor Fertig dyed herself, draped across the bare walls and homemade seats. Mona told others that she had several good teachers, notably Mr. R.L. Maher and Miss A.K. Hill—no first names in those days. Mr. Maher taught her English, Journalism, Creative Writing and Photography.

Looking back at her life for this book from Salt Spring Island, off the coast of B.C., Fertig recalls with laughter:

I started writing poetry in Grade 6, 1965. By Grade 10, I was writing poetry like crazy, and a group of us in the Journalism class took over designing the school annual: I put my poems and drawings in it, and we put every student under their astrological signs. That was so much fun.[15]

Miss Hill taught Art, which besides drawing and some painting, included learning the popular hippie crafts of the day, batik and tie-dyeing techniques, god's eyes, basket and belt weaving and candle making.

Fertig remembers reading the lyrics of Leonard Cohen's "Suzanne" and in grade ten compiled her own first book-art piece, "Illustrations of Poems," patching together its imitation leather cover and sewing in her own watercolour illustrated pages of Canadian band Steppenwolf's 1968 hit "Born to Be Wild," along with "The Fool on the Hill" and "Give a Damn."

Vancouver by the late '60s was one of North America's counterculture bastions, along with San Francisco, New York, Toronto and Montreal. Fertig, though, was not quite old enough for the city's original 4th Avenue scene in Kitsilano or its music venues that were cohesive in keeping the alternative scene alive—the Afterthought, Retinal Circus, Village Bistro and others. Fertig muses:

I didn't really know what was going on in the poetry or music scene in Vancouver at that time. But I knew what was happening in the art scene through the discussions my parents would have with various artist friends who came to visit and by my father's struggle to find a gallery to show his work and sell paintings (as well as his raku pottery). I knew the artists' names but not the writers.[16]

It was poet Beth Jankola, the Fertigs' Burnaby neighbour, who brought Mona an awareness of Vancouver's poetry scene. Jankola had a beatnik air, wore black beat-era clothing and had met Mona's mother Evelyn while both worked at the *Vancouver Sun*. The Jankolas had known the Fertigs in Kitsilano, and Beth had been influenced by

George's and Evelyn's discussions about art and psychology; she would later emerge as a painter in her own right.[17] A few years later when Beth became aware of her young neighbour's interest in poetry, she began inviting Mona to join her at reading events. Tooling off to the city in Jankola's green Volkswagen Beetle, the pair attended many readings at the Advance Mattress coffeehouse on 4th Avenue where Milton Acorn had organized events,[18] and where Mona encountered the gifted poet Pat Lowther, as well as Kitsilano's bookstores, parks and communal houses. In this way, Fertig gained her early sense of what was happening in the city's poetry culture. She worked seriously at the craft herself. Eileen Kernaghan recalls her entering several poems in the Burnaby Writers' Society contest and winning when Fertig was still seventeen.[19]

It would be Beth Jankola who'd bring a library book over to Mona one day that told the extraordinary story of Sylvia Beach, an American expatriate in Paris who founded Shakespeare and Company, the legendary Left Bank bookshop and informal literary centre after World War I. Fertig read the book, and it marked a pivotal moment in her life. Remarkable things could be done by ordinary people—by women—she realized, without money or celebrity. It was an epiphany that would send out ripples in a wide-reaching arc. But while a new idea based on Sylvia Beach's historic shop germinated inside her, ducking into pubs with Jankola was a more taboo pastime. Fertig recalls:

I could get into the Cecil Pub with fake ID when I was underage. I'd hang out there with Beth and other older poets. I was seventeen, probably the youngest person in the place. Beth was about twenty years older. All the poets would head there after readings.[20]

After learning that a group of poets met regularly at the Vancouver Public Library (VPL) in its then Burrard and Robson Street location, Fertig followed up on the information. It was there that she first met Tim Lander, Ed Varney, Nellie McClung and Cathy Ford who would become a life-long friend.

From the winter of 1972 until the spring of 1974, these downtown poets used the library space to meet and to read their poems, and in 1974 started the Vancouver Poetry Co-op, which aimed to publish members' books at Intermedia Press. The group comprised Beth Jankola, Tim Lander, Nellie McClung, Gwen Hauser, Ed Varney, Cathy Ford, Roger Perkins, Wain Ewing, Vince Chetcuti, Richard Lemm, Roger Prentice, Alan Muckle and Avron Hoffman.[21] Other poets like Eric Ivan Berg joined in later. "Poetic Licences" were issued. Ed Varney recalls:

The meetings at the library came right after a poetry reading series there that I organized. It included many of the same poets—bill bissett, myself, Henry Rappaport, Avron Hoffman, Jim Carter, Maxine Gadd, Judy Copithorne, etc. I also found the bindery at the VPL to be very helpful in learning how to do hard-bound books.

The VPL meetings were mini poetry readings; anyone could come and read their work. There was little, if any, discussion about the work or about poetics. It was very egalitarian. I met a lot of new poets at the meetings, and it was also an opportunity to keep in touch with old friends and what they were doing.[22]

In 1972 Fertig was eighteen when she met her first actual poetry teacher. Judith Copithorne had run a writers' workshop since the early 1970s at her storefront premises home on 2165 Yew Street between 5th and 6th Avenues in Kitsilano. Painters Frank Molnar, Jack Akroyd and Joan Payne kept studios there too. Fertig visited the storefront site with Beth and attended poetry workshops run by Copithorne, who came from a family that had worked for the pioneering socialist CCF government in Saskatchewan. From the cooperative, mainly farming background of its constituency, Copithorne had learned ideas of social development that went back to Robert Owen.

It was a fantastic opportunity for a young writer. "Judith published *Returning II* and some little magazines," Fertig observes. "She produced a number of issues. I had my first poetry published in it.

What I remember is all the women poets."[23]

Fertig then went on to self-publish her first book, *The Elusive Unicorn*, in 1972 by following Jankola's lead. She took her poetry to the Workers' Compensation Board where injured workers handset 100 copies of 14 poems on old presses for free as this was part of their work rehabilitation.[24]

I drew a cover and stapled the poems together and bound the chapbook with coloured tape. My father then took me to Duthie Books where I was introduced to Binky Marks, and he happily put some copies on the shelf in the poetry section to sell.

Vancouver was a much smaller city than it is today. Coming from the Prairies where people were used to thinking and behaving more progressively, both socially and politically, Judith Copithorne had found that, in Vancouver during the 1960s,

some of the young male artists and a few of the [veteran] male writers were inclined to be somewhat arrogant. You sometimes had young men who perhaps came from the smaller towns, or who didn't have as much of an intellectual background as those who had grown up in the cities with more exposure to a range of intellectual and political ideas. Some of the younger artists and a few of the poets hadn't heard of Gertrude Stein or Simone de Beauvoir; they were not activists. Women were around to be decorative and helpful. When male artists realized that women wanted a piece of the pie, they got antsy. By the 1970s there was a kind of backlash.[25]

Copithorne's women's writing workshop was unique but sui generis—of its time. She recalls:

Claire Stannard, Shana Fox, Beth Jankola and perhaps Mariko Kiyooka came, as did Mona and several others . . . It was an already brilliant group of youngsters. Beth had been writing for a good long while, as well as bringing up a family, and had some wonderful design ideas as well. She was an important addition to the group. The younger people were also very talented, and considering how young they were, each had a fair amount of experience and knowledge in the fields of literature and writing. Then, as always, Mona was a very inner-directed and outwardly giving young woman. I would think that what she got from that workshop mostly was being with those other young women who were all quite inspired.[26]

As David Watmough contends, the conditions for women writers of the times were mixed at best, if not lousy.

Look back at those times: there was a sense of separation between men and women. We've had real advances in cultural equality, including the gay movement . . . Poets had a harder time of it, especially women. First they were women, then writers, then poets. That's a three-time whammy. There were a lot of very good poets scattered about Vancouver; however, the men were more easily institutionalized. Where, for instance, was the female counterpart to Earle Birney?[27]

Fertig was not yet fully conscious of the politics within the literary community where, as Blanche Howard argued, "women were acknowledged as being among Canada's most admired writers, yet they were still treated as a minority interest in the field of reviews."[28]

"There were a lot of male writers, and I knew that they were in charge," Fertig says. "I spent time with some of the women writers—Gwen Hauser was there, Rosalind Smythe, Cathy Ford, Beth Jankola, Colette Connor, Helen Potrebenko. You'd go to readings, and they'd be there. Then I began organizing readings myself when I was eighteen."

Shortly before graduating high school in 1972, she became involved peripherally with Intermedia, the Vancouver artists' cooperative that operated between 1965 and 1971. Cathy Ford recalls:

Intermedia Society eventually evolved into Intermedia Press, with Ed Varney and Henry Rappaport at the helm, learning to print, publish, promote all types of materials from postcards, to posters, to broadsides, to poetry books, to anthologies, to trade titles. People entered the revolving door—to learn, to help out, to volunteer, to edit, to design, to create cover and commercial work. Painters, poets, printers, all fell together up the stairs, into a huge open space with light tables, printers, guillotines, computer typeset machines. People would arrive with projects they wanted to accomplish, and many of us worked for free or nearly so, it was all so close to the line, creating publishing and printed artworks, until it became more of a business. Important things in the literary history of Vancouver were created over lunch, in wild and wide-ranging discussions, and the open atmosphere that prevailed for many years.[29]

Ed Varney,
Intermedia Press, 1972.
Photograph courtesy of
Henry Rappaport

After graduating and winning an arts award for her raku ceramics and large wall batiks, Mona attended a summer arts school on Columbia Street in New Westminster, which was beginning its decline following the opening of a large shopping mall nearby.

That summer she began attending travelling arts and crafts fairs in Mission and Courtenay, where she sold her father's raku pottery and her own batik dresses, T-shirts and poetry. She also secured employment from the Vancouver Parks Board teaching arts and crafts to children. It was rewarding work and continued into the fall with an instructor's post at the Hillside Boys and Girls Club in suburban Delta. There she used the office Gestetner machine to print *Bittergreen* on blue and green paper. It was her second self-published poetry chapbook.

In high school, Fertig had planned on enrolling at UBC after graduation, to possibly become an art teacher. She had even taken French, a subject she disliked, in order to qualify for the program, but her family lacked the money to send her to university. With this realization, she turned to art school.[30]

In 1973 her portfolio of drawings, linocuts and other artwork gained her entry in the Vancouver School of Art. She was living in Kitsilano by then, in shared housing. She studied the basic first-year syllabus that included drawing, graphic design, silversmithing and a "dull art history course" taught by Ian Wallace. Geoff Rees who taught Design was her favourite teacher. Fertig enjoyed the opportunity to hang out with the city's emerging visual and performance artists, and dressed flamboyantly in red, purple and black.[31] She recalls that year with enthusiasm: "I had a fantastic time," she remembers with a sinful grin. "I loved printmaking." She befriended fellow art students Sid Morozoff, Trudi Forrest,[32] Fiona McKye[33] and Danny Kostyshin.[34]

But by the summer of 1974, she left the school. The first of her adult epiphanies had arrived: "After a year, I felt art school wasn't for me. I knew that I was really a poet."

Out of her growing encounters with other poets, Fertig became more invested in the Vancouver Poetry Co-op and published her first full-length book, *Seasons That I Am*.[35] She shared the group's collective desire to create a centre for poetry. By 1975 she was producing *Vancouver Poetry*, a weekly radio program for the cooperative radio station CFRO, from its Hastings Street-Gastown area studios. Her mother also volunteered at the station as a receptionist at the front desk and handled the phones and co-op information, as she would later do at the Literary Storefront. Others involved at CFRO included the literary journalist Hal Wake, who would work for the CBC and later succeed Alma Lee as director of the Vancouver Writers Festival, as well as Eleanor Wachtel (currently the host of *Writers and Company*, CBC Radio), Norbert Reubsaat, Howard Broomfield and Ingrid Klassen, creator of the ground-breaking locally focused *The Book Show*.

"I don't know where this idea of gathering people together came from, since I was quite shy and quiet," Fertig notes. Whatever the case, as a natural extension of the meetings at the library, one of the first grants she applied for with the Vancouver Poetry Co-op group was to establish a poetry centre in Chinatown. By that time, the group had developed a program of the kind of work and creative community-building it wished to accomplish.

Fertig relates:

I was to be the Program Coordinator, Beth Jankola, Gwen Hauser, Tim Lander and Nellie McClung were to be the Poet Workers, plus there was to be a secretary/bookkeeper. The Poetry Co-op Resource Center would serve as an informal meeting place for poets and writers as well as an archive and coordinating center to promote interaction between poets and the community.[36]

The Poetry Co-op also had a site in mind. They were interested in the slim shop-front premises at the corner of Columbia and Pender, popularly known as "the thinnest store in the world."[37] Fertig and her colleagues hosted several readings there, finding it a wonderful place to read, and looked into leasing the space.[38] As the Vancouver Poetry Co-op, Fertig and friends applied for $17,780 to open the Vancouver Poetry Co-op Resource Center.[39] Letters of support came from George Whiten, the veteran community organizer and director of the Neighbourhood Services Association, and from Ed Varney, director of the Poem Company, Gregg Simpson of Intermedia Press, Dorothy Metcalfe who was Special Events Coordinator at the Vancouver Art Gallery, and D.M. Fraser of Pulp Press.

Despite the federal government's largesse in doling out funds from

WEST COAST POETS

THIS FALL AT THE
VANCOUVER PUBLIC LIBRARY
750 BURRARD STREET
☆ SUNDAY AFTERNOONS ☆
2:30 - 3:30
FREE

OCTOBER 17th
BRIAN BRETT, NELLIE McCLUNG & ALLAN SAFARIK

OCTOBER 24th
PAT LANE & MONA FERTIG

OCTOBER 31st
BETH JANKOLA & PETER TROWER

NOVEMBER 7th
SUSAN MUSGRAVE & FRED CANDELARIA

NOVEMBER 14th
GLADYS HINDMARCH & HENRY RAPPAPORT

NOVEMBER 21st
LIONEL KEARNS & MARYA FIAMENGO

NOVEMBER 28th
DAPHNE MARLATT, CAROLE ITTER & EDWIN VARNEY

DECEMBER 5th
HELENE ROSENTHAL & CATHY FORD

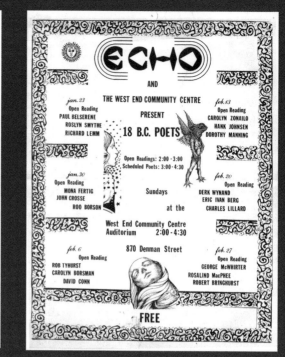

ECHO

AND

THE WEST END COMMUNITY CENTRE
PRESENT
18 B.C. POETS

jan. 23
Open Reading
PAUL BELSERENE
ROSLYN SMYTHE
RICHARD LEMM

feb. 13
Open Reading
CAROLYN ZONAILO
HANK JOHNSEN
DOROTHY MANNING

Open Readings: 2:00 - 3:00
Scheduled Poets: 3:00 - 4:30

jan. 30
Open Reading
MONA FERTIG
JOHN CROSSE
ROO BORSON

Sundays

feb. 20
Open Reading
DERK WYNAND
ERIC IVAN BERG
CHARLES LILLARD

at the

West End Community Centre
Auditorium   2:00 - 4:30

870 Denman Street

feb. 6
Open Reading
ROB TYHURST
CAROLYN BORSMAN
DAVID CONN

feb. 27
Open Reading
GEORGE McWHIRTER
ROSALIND MacPHEE
ROBERT BRINGHURST

FREE

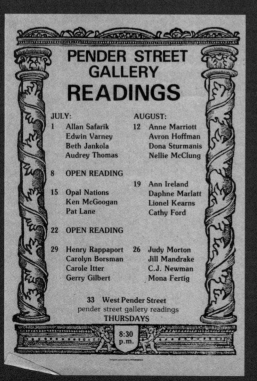

PENDER STREET GALLERY
READINGS

JULY:
1   Allan Safarik
    Edwin Varney
    Beth Jankola
    Audrey Thomas

8   OPEN READING

15 Opal Nations
    Ken McGoogan
    Pat Lane

22 OPEN READING

29 Henry Rappaport
    Carolyn Borsman
    Carole Itter
    Gerry Gilbert

AUGUST:
12 Anne Marriott
    Avron Hoffman
    Dona Sturmanis
    Nellie McClung

19 Ann Ireland
    Daphne Marlatt
    Lionel Kearns
    Cathy Ford

26 Judy Morton
    Jill Mandrake
    C.J. Newman
    Mona Fertig

33 West Pender Street
pender street gallery readings
THURSDAYS

8:30 p.m.

THURSDAY EVENING

SEPT 9   marguerite and alan NEIL

SEPT 16 david uu & isle of avalon society

SEPT 23 gladys HINDMARCH

SEPT 30 bill bissett

OCT 7   gerry GILBERT

OCT 14   george BOWERING

POETRY READINGS

BAU-XI GALLERY
555 hamilton, Van.
doors close at 8:30

the Local Initiatives Program, or LIP grants, in the early 1970s, the group's application was not successful.[40]

In 1975 Fertig met Peter Haase, an electrician and musician from Liverpool. Haase came to Canada in 1971, after four years in Australia, and settled in Vancouver after a look at Toronto and a year in the Yukon. He earned a living as an electrician and sang evenings at pubs and clubs. They met late one evening on the Granville Street bus; it was the Ides of March. Peter had played at the King's Head Pub near Kitsilano Beach and planned to join friends in Gastown; when he came outside, his car had been towed away. He caught the bus instead.

Mona was the first writer Peter had ever met. She showed him an unbound proof of her new book of poetry, *Seasons That I Am,* that she drew from her bag. It had arrived from the publisher that very day. They had a cup of tea together at Denny's restaurant on Broadway.

Taken by the intensity of Mona's engagement with the literary community and her radio program, Haase became her main supporter and frequently helped set up technical equipment for the program's live on-air broadcasts from studios A and B, or via live phone hookups from other places, such as the Vancouver Public Library or a gallery. Between poets, he'd sing a tune to punctuate performances.

Haase soon moved into a small house next door to the Jankola family and worked through the Industrial Brotherhood of Electrical Workers. After a cross-Canada driving and camping trip, Mona joined Peter in the little house, where they had garden parties with writers and musicians on their quarter-acre. She continued to organize readings in Vancouver with the library group, and independently at virtually every library and gallery in Vancouver and Burnaby. The idea that had first blossomed when Beth Jankola had dropped over with *Shakespeare and Company* was also still resonating in her mind. It began taking form as a hybrid concept. Mona reflects:

I had heard of the Canada Council Explorations grants. Funding

Vancouver reading posters, 1970s

was awarded to "the introduction of something new or different in the sphere of social understanding or the means of fostering public enjoyment of cultural activities or our Canadian heritage." So in May of 1977, I sat down and wrote an application for a project based on the idea of Shakespeare & Company in Paris.[41]

Initial letters of support came from Fred Candelaria, Professor of English at Simon Fraser University; Mrs. Burnett, the Head Librarian at Vancouver Public Library; and Elisa Anstis, Curator at the Burnaby Art Gallery. The purpose of "Shakespeare and Company," which was the original name on the application, was to "encourage the serious study and development of Canadian writers." Other support letters arrived from Susan Musgrave, Roy Kiyooka and Daphne Marlatt, bill bissett, Judith Copithorne, the Poetry Project in New York, the Burnaby Public Library, Eric Ivan Berg, the Makara Collective, Press Gang, *Room of One's Own* and others.

Stephen Osborne of Pulp Press, now the award-winning publisher and editor-in-chief of *Geist* magazine, contributed an additional outstanding letter to the Canada Council:

What we lack here is the community sense of writing which exists in such centres as Toronto ... To some extent [Mona] will be taking up the slack caused by the gradual diminition [*sic*] over the years, of interest and cooperation by such groups as the Western Front which increasingly cater to more and more sophisticated artists at the expense (literally) of local, young, striving, often extremely talented writers and artists ... Pulp Press workers feel that her goal is sane and credible; all national art and literature, after all, only grows out of particular places, regions, sensibilities. Thus we encourage you to assist Mona Fertig in her request for funds.[42]

Mona's Literary Storefront idea was for a place open to everyone, from emerging writers to readers, as well as the established and well-known. She intuited that her instinct for this kind of level playing field came from observing her father's struggles against elitism in the art world. Years later, she was able to acknowledge how "certain poets, regarded me as naïve, which I was. But I was determined that I would make my own way, create my own space, because I believed in myself."

Fertig had developed an ability to gather people and wanted to use this to make a statement, to open things right up. She sensed that writers wanted and needed to come together:

Part of me was so young and passionate, yet part was also intuitively much wiser than I knew. Writers and artists work alone, and I love that part, working by myself; and then I like to be with the collective, where we bounce ideas off each other, feel stimulated listening to other people's work, then go home to our rooms and write. For me it was like food.

Fertig submitted her grant application and waited for a response. While she waited, a stroke of luck arrived when she was hired on a separate grant-funded basis as an education and special events coordinator by the Surrey Arts Centre for the Surrey Art Gallery. Situated in the province's largest municipality, the gallery was committed to enhancing the role of culture in an area that was transitioning from its rural roots to growing suburban importance. At Bear Creek Park off the King George Highway, it was located mid-point between expanding residential sub-divisions and Surrey's traditional southern farmlands.

With her family's background in art and her own first year's experience at art school, Fertig brought inspired energy with her. She loved and was successful at the new community outreach job. The director of the Surrey Art Gallery was Lorna Farrell-Ward, who later became a curator and acting director at the Vancouver Art Gallery for a year. The supervisor of the Surrey Arts Centre was Linette Wright Smith, who has remained a friend ever since. Farrell-Ward had a distinct sense of the young administrator she was hiring.[43] "I always thought you were the best in bringing home what you believe in," she said in an email to Fertig:

As far as Surrey... I heard you on the radio near Christmas and knew you were right for a position I was thinking about. In the '70s, community art galleries just showed art, perhaps with art classes. I wanted to bring the best we could from outside the community as well as locally, and include a context for exhibitions to show that they did not exist in isolation. Your grant was one of the first to come through when it was difficult, and was a very important one to start the process. It increased the support of the municipality . . . In addition to supporting writers, we were able to have workshops and programs for the schools.[44]

Farrell-Ward's confidence was well-founded. While at the Surrey Arts Centre, Fertig organized many special events; one was a major West Coast Writers' Festival the weekend of October 29-30, 1977. It featured a tremendous line-up of B.C. writers.[i] There were workshops on bookbinding; calligraphy, how to print your own books, children and poetry; as well as live music and hot food and a display and history of current B.C. literary magazines and periodicals in the theatre gallery. The readings were taped by Co-op Radio. Farrell-Ward remembers Susan Musgrave coming to see her to tell her how much the West Coast Writers' Festival meant to her.

Fertig also organized workshop kits for the schools: "Life Rhythms," a "History of Early and Modern Pottery and Sculpture" with Christa Preus; "Japanese Culture" led by the Powell Street Revue; as well as a "Canadian Painting" workshop; another on "West Coast Indians"; and Reinhold Visuals kits that assisted in the teaching of art.

Mona travelled daily from Burnaby to her Surrey Arts Centre job. Despite her pleasure in the challenges of the work, its temporal nature and the necessity of a long drive through three municipalities,

---

i   Appearing were Cam Hubert, Jack Hodgins, D.M. Fraser, Brett Enemark, Brian Brett, Eleanor Crowe, Maxine Gadd, Myra MacFarlane, Nellie McClung, Marya Fiamengo, Robert Bringhurst, Hank Johnsen, Susan Musgrave, Fred Candelaria, The Vancouver Poetry Quartet, Leona Gom, Tom Wayman, Helen Potrebenko, bill bissett, Cathy Ford, Leona Gom, Gerry Gilbert, Beth Jankola, Tim Lander, John Pass, Roger Prentice, Andreas Schroeder, Dona Sturmanis and Carolyn Zonailo. .

she was unsettled regarding career directions. What she needed was to make money in a position that felt like a steady job. She was in readiness position for a change.

Fertig occasionally looks back on the moment when she heard that her Explorations application made the cut. She was notified of the grant while she was still employed by the Surrey Arts Centre and now had a serious choice to make about her path in life. She decided to follow her bliss.

Almost simultaneously, the gallery contacted her with news that the Surrey municipality had made her position, and that of several others, permanent. "I could've had a pension!" Fertig laughs. Ingrid Kolt, the woman who succeeded Fertig, would stay on for decades.

In her Explorations application, Fertig had requested $8,400. On September 15, 1977, a letter from Charles Lussier, Director at the Canada Council, informed Fertig that $7,500 funding for an eight-month project would be granted in two disbursements. A series of letter exchanges with Burke Taylor, Head of Explorations Program at the Council, followed, in which Fertig explained she was still employed at the Surrey Art Gallery but would be leaving in the spring. Could her grant commence April 1, 1978 instead of January 1, 1978?

From the moment she received notice of the funds, for what she would now call "The Literary Storefront," Fertig began sending out press notices from her desk at home. Then on February 1, 1978, the *Capilano Courier* reported, "Yes it's true. For once, beautiful but backward B.C. is scoring a first over the rest of Canada. In May, [its] first literary storefront will be opening."[45]

Fertig understood that the Canada Council couldn't fund a bookshop per se. Her ideal business model remained a type of non-profit contemporary literary centre based on the auxiliary activities that had taken place at Sylvia Beach's store in Paris, as well as other models she had since learned more about, including Frances Steloff's Gotham Book Mart in New York and Lawrence Ferlinghetti's City

Clockwise from upper left:
George Fertig, Peter Haase
Peter Haase and volunteer
Cathy Ford, Jane Munro
Evelyn Fertig
John Warren, Peter Haase

Lights Books in San Francisco. It would be, she imagined, a hub for grassroots activity, as well as a modern space for all kinds of writers. What Vancouver needed in the late '70s, she reckoned, was an antidote to a literary scene that was "fragmented by many different writing cliques, schools and university groups all rolling around in their own universe."[46]

Accordingly, she got busy making lists, gathering notes about who could help, applying for Canada Council readings by Earle Birney, Dorothy Livesay and others, and searching for a suitable location in the Chinatown-Gastown area. The thinnest building was too small and no longer available. Jane Rule wrote her, "I wish you success for your storefront salon. Longhouse in Toronto and The Double Hook in Montreal are such welcoming places to drop in and it would be marvelous to have something of the sort in Vancouver."[47]

A friend, likely Lorna Farrell-Ward, recommended that she contact Marathon Realty, a division of the Canadian Pacific Railway that administered its extensive property holdings. Gastown was situated adjacent to the CPR's huge downtown Vancouver marshalling yards, so Fertig and Haase approached Marathon and explained her search for a suitable location for a literary centre at an affordable rent. The company agreed to let her have a vacant second-floor dress shop with a set of changing rooms at #213-131 Water Street. Rent was a bargain at $275 monthly, including heat, water and air conditioning. The area was being promoted as "Gaslight Square." Fertig was offered the lease on April 15, 1978. Things were getting close.

Fertig understood that what the Literary Storefront would need was people. On April 21, the *Province* newspaper's Callboard announced, "Persons interested in volunteering or donating materials are asked to call 433-8041." Peter Haase recalls:

We scored a great group of volunteers who helped set us up in the very beginning. They pitched in at several working-bees, and this big empty storefront with huge air-conditioning ducts and

CITY LIGHTS
BOOKSELLERS & PUBLISHERS
261 COLUMBUS AVENUE
SAN FRANCISCO, CALIF. 94133

POST CARD

PLACE
STAMP
HERE

PHOTO: © 1973 WALTER CHAPPELL. COURTESY AMSTRA...

Good Luck

— Lawrence Ferlinghetti

water pipes overhead was converted. We went in there and dusted it down, painted the whole thing beautifully. It had a couple of nice brick walls on the side, and we later sold membership bricks—you got your name in gold, letterset on a little cream card and glued to the brick and that was *your* brick, right?[48]

Mucking in alongside Fertig, her family and Haase, volunteers included Sheila McCarthy, Peter Goodchild, Cathy Ford, Dwain Ruckle, John Warren, Jane Munro and Jennifer Alley. In comradely fashion, they repainted the old dress shop's garish orange walls in a fresh cream tone, erected shelves, solicited donations of office furniture and equipment and, in what would become a Literary Storefront working-bee trademark, drank beer and ate chili and pizza while finishing up the job.

Within two weeks, all was ready. Fertig was able to distribute the invitations she'd illustrated on vivid green paper, accompanied by a press release that announced the opening of a new literary centre. In tribute to Sylvia Beach, Fertig commissioned fabric artist Sima Elizabeth Shefrin to make a life-size soft sculpture of the Storefront's inspiring spirit for the grand opening.[49] The perky rag doll Sylvia would preside over Storefront activities for years.

With the cleanup and fresh coat of paint accomplished, the Literary Storefront, Mona Fertig and her supporters were ready to roll and tumble.

Invitation to Literary Storefront opening, May 13, 1978

Mona Fertig
Photograph by Glenn Baglo/Vancouver Sun

2

1978: Gathering Together, the Big Opening

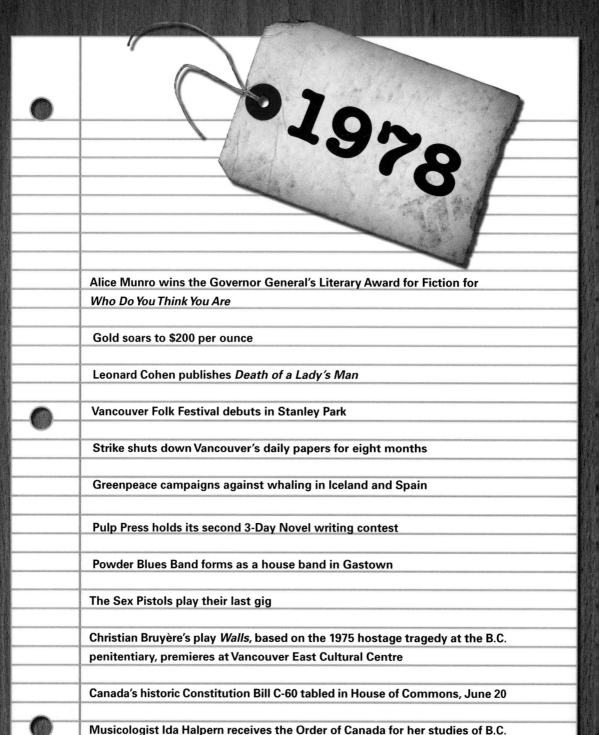

1978

Alice Munro wins the Governor General's Literary Award for Fiction for
Who Do You Think You Are

Gold soars to $200 per ounce

Leonard Cohen publishes *Death of a Lady's Man*

Vancouver Folk Festival debuts in Stanley Park

Strike shuts down Vancouver's daily papers for eight months

Greenpeace campaigns against whaling in Iceland and Spain

Pulp Press holds its second 3-Day Novel writing contest

Powder Blues Band forms as a house band in Gastown

The Sex Pistols play their last gig

Christian Bruyère's play *Walls*, based on the 1975 hostage tragedy at the B.C.
penitentiary, premieres at Vancouver East Cultural Centre

Canada's historic Constitution Bill C-60 tabled in House of Commons, June 20

Musicologist Ida Halpern receives the Order of Canada for her studies of B.C.
First Nations' music

The Literary Storefront officially opened its doors on May 13, 1978. Thirty-seven years on, Fertig can muse, "I don't know where all the energy came from." Her family came by to help, with her mother, Evelyn, joining other volunteers in painting the former dress shop. Peter Haase, by now her life partner, pitched in too, working long hours alongside Mona. He would become a steadfast supporter of Mona and her projects. Her mother then volunteered to answer the phones and enquiries a half day per week. George, the introverted father, called in from time to time. Both parents were startled by their previously shy daughter's achievement. Mona remembers:

An old high-school friend and my sister Moana helped prepare the food on opening night. What was important was the vision for the place, that it wasn't just another closed space. I wanted to welcome all kinds of literary ideas; be open to everyone.

Given the times, it was inevitable that some in the city's arts community assumed Fertig was too young, too idealistic, insufficiently academically educated or that there was no burgeoning literary scene to lead. "I've come to see that sometimes there are people who are just too focused on their own authority," Fertig smiles. "I wasn't going to wait for permission." She concludes:

It wasn't just about showcasing well-known or famous writers. I wanted the inexperienced writers, women writers, the closet writers all mingling—inspiring a real ferment for ideas and action. Sylvia Beach opened a small bookshop, and then she's publishing James Joyce and *Ulysses*; I wanted things like that to happen. A sociological/literary combustion. Salon-style. Grassroots.

Among media notices that preceded the opening, two would illustrate conventional prejudices against this new approach. A lukewarm article by Carol Read that appeared in the *Ubyssey* student newspaper at UBC revealed how far campus attitudes had drifted during the late '70s from the activist decade previous, intimating that Fertig's populist grounding was regarded by the student reporter as insufficiently "academic" or tony enough for the times—presumably for student journalists and readers seeking careers in British colonial administration. The conservative-oriented *Province*, while noting the long odds against an idea such as Fertig's, also offered a rare, first-person endorsement from Barrie Cook, reporting, "It's an idealistic, illogical, incredible marvelous idea and I sincerely hope it works."[50]

The opening night invitation read:

In the tradition of the famous literary salons and bookshops of Paris, London, New York and San Fransisco. You are invited to the Grand Opening of Canada's first Literary Storefront. Bring your dancing shoes, and a book to contribute to our library.

The typo did not go unnoticed by the literary police:

In my excitement I misspelled San Francisco and one well-known male Vancouver poet circled the spelling mistake and returned the invite to the Canada Council with the comment, "Just thought you'd be glad to know that your money is well-spent in furtherance of Canada's literate culture." The Canada Council felt I should be made aware of this person and mailed me the comment advising me to watch my back. I was angry about this, but not wholly surprised. This attitude of elitism was exactly the reason we needed the Literary Storefront. Needless to say, I never invited this poet to read.[51]

On opening night, over 200 poets, writers, editors, publishers, booksellers and friends turned up to celebrate. Publisher Jack Mc-Clelland sent an encouraging letter from Toronto, explaining, "Sorry I can not manage to attend the opening of your Literary Storefront. It sounds exciting and imaginative. I hope it was a great success."[52] Fertig invited Geoff Hancock, editor of *Canadian Fiction Magazine*, to officially open the Literary Storefront.[53]

Mona asked me, a young literary editor of a short story magazine, to make a little speech and cut the pages of a book as official opening of her new Literary Storefront . . . That rainy night I put on my best red and blue hand-knitted artsy yarn necktie, headed out in the sluic-

ing rain . . . Her combined drop-in centre, non-traditional non-profit combo book and artshop, with an ambitious side of newsletter [and] pamphlets about the art and business of writing and publishing appealed to my sense of process, discovery, permeables, and variables. Mona had a romantic faith in the open-ended possibilities of art and literature, not as static but flowing and dynamic.[54]

Then the party began. Marathon Realty allowed the new tenants to use the empty unfinished upstairs space for dancing. You got there only by elevator. The large room full of windows and cement pillars had a small outside balcony. Fertig and Haase set up an Akai reel-to-reel with three hours of great music on each reel, Peter ran the bar.

Interior of Storefront, #213-131 Water Street, Gaslight Square

He had twenty cases of Labatt Blue donated and delivered for free because he'd told Labatt's there was a big literary event taking place. It was a wonderful night of dancing, drinking and smoking.

The press release for the launch said it all and set out the work plan for the next five years:

Projected activities include workshops, readings, lectures, exhibitions, films, courses, and special events. There will also be a [Sylvia Beach and Adrienne Monnier inspired] member's lending library, private study areas, a writers-in-residence programme and resource information available . . . Hours are 10-6 PM Tuesday-Saturday and some Sundays and evenings—I would like to thank everyone who has given their support, from the first letters to Explorations spring 1977, to the finishing touches opening night.

We did it!

The *Vancouver Sun* covered the gala with a full-page article, "Literary Den Mother," by Scott Macrae, June 2, 1978:

If ingenuous enthusiasm equals success, Fertig is teetering giddily on the brink . . . Much of the energy of Shakespeare and Company was created by the spontaneous comings and goings of the literati. The problem is: how to organically nurture literature when the poet is as much concerned about expense vouchers as iambic pentameter?

Macrae, one of the city's best arts writers, had already seen a letter written to the newspaper by a self-appointed critic taking a pre-emptive swing. An unkind response to Fertig's effort, it dismissed the Storefront-soon-to-be as "a rather personal cart-before-the horse nostalgia trip . . . about as suited to the New World as an English pub."[55] Macrae the journalist, however, maintained a funkily respectful attitude, noting, "[Fertig] guesses, yes, that she may be a child of the grant culture," but infers this is okay. Writing in a mode brought to the city's big daily newspaper by wildman countercultural columnist Bob Hunter, who had also been the formative energy in launching Greenpeace, Macrae concluded in Alice-in-Wonderland fashion, "Happy Fertig, cosmic Fertig, smiles. She just knows the place will work out."

Water Street, Gastown, 1975, Photograph by William E. Graham,
Vancouver Archives CVA 1135-60

3

Life and Times in
Gastown's Bohemia

During the reign of Pierre Trudeau's federal Liberals, heritage renovation funding was generous, and Gastown was undergoing a transformation as its red-brick, light-industrial and extensive clothing-trade warehouses began morphing into Vancouver's tourist-oriented "Old Town" strip. The British Columbia New Democratic Party under leader Dave Barrett had finally relaxed the province's notoriously Protestant drinking laws, and Gastown's Water Street and numerous side crossings came alive with a flourishing pub trade that put the city's traditional hotel drinking saloons in the deep shade. The Spinning Wheel, Blarney Stone, Medieval Inn, Harp and Heather: these were the new places to have fun and get a bit giddy.

"Vancouver's arts scene was vibrant at that time," Peter Haase recollects.[56] "You could walk through the streets of Gastown, and there was always something going on—readings, artwork, street musicians, all sorts. It reminded me of London in the late '60s to early '70s."

At the time of the Literary Storefront's emergence, Vancouver was a creative touchstone for writers who made their way there from all over Canada. Bill Jeffries, an independent visual arts curator and artist who founded the Coburg Gallery in 1983, across the hall from the Literary Storefront at its second Gastown location, remembers this as "a fairly optimistic time with a lot of stuff going on."[57] Although creatively rich, it could be a contrary place at the same time, such as when Robin Blaser was heckled at the Vancouver Poetry Society's "Free Speech Party" at the UBC Student Union Building ballroom on December 29, 1978. [58]

Poet Carolyn Zonailo had recently finished university and was working to fashion a career in writing and, she recalls, possibly publishing. Access was a challenge, and while contacts could be made with older established figures in the arts, it could still be difficult to translate this into a place from which to launch specific projects. The Storefront was a new beginning, a welcoming place as she remembers:

The Literary Storefront was our Paris in Vancouver—what excitement! It was the number one gathering place for local and visiting writers . . . The L.S. was founded by a woman, Mona Fertig, who had a vision of Vancouver more worldly in scope than the actual Vancouver of that time.[59]

Not only was the West Coast scene ripe for a new literary space, but it needed one as a locus for literary activity somewhere between the hermetic self-absorption of the universities and colleges, the niche experimentalists and the one-off readings in bookstores, galleries and the taprooms of tenderloin pubs. Gordon Cornwall, now a retired software entrepreneur, remembers the boxed-in feeling younger novice writers like him felt at the time:

I got interested in the Storefront early, about a year after Mona got started. I began dropping in shortly after the move to Cordova Street. I read there once, something funny. There didn't seem to be anywhere else to read. There was the Western Front, home of the avant garde, which for some was hard to find entry into. In those days, the Storefront was mostly local writers, Canadian writers, young writers. I was interested because I was trying to write myself. I'd done a PhD in Philosophy that didn't lead to a career, and I had literary stuff going on the side, but I was hitting the usual wall in getting it published.[60]

What this meant was that newer, committed writers needed ways to get plugged in. The general social and working conditions for writers at the time were, as Dona Sturmanis—then a recent graduate from UBC's Creative Writing program—recalls:

Very activist . . . lots of poverty, poetry, politics, publishing and perseverance. It was the best of times, the worst of times . . . extremely creative, very literary-oriented. Conditions for women writers at the time were not great . . . a very male-dominated scene with the women trying to break through.[61]

Sturmanis is echoed by Cathy Ford who writes:

Some of us became friends for life by tackling the most pressing social, economic, political, sexist, racist, classist subject at hand, and

Mona at work

working together on a project . . . What we all had in common [was] energy to change things, to open access to writing and publishing, especially for the vibrant women's writing all around us, and lots and lots of coffee and earnest discussions about one another's work and reading and childhoods, and most of all, writing, obsessions. While trying to get some of our own work done! [62]

The Storefront's first official day of operation as Canada's first non-profit literary centre was Tuesday, May 16. The anomaly and dazzle of having a literary centre in Vancouver became an attractor force, and as Mona Fertig, founder and director, began to organize a myriad literary events, other ideas gradually came from local writers and publishers looking for opportunities and occasions to become involved. The Storefront's first regular event came on its second day of business with a reading by eastern poet Claude Liman at 8 PM. Its first weekend marked the beginning of Open Space, a Sunday evening open-mic session where writers like me could get a sense of what reading to an audience was like.

Months of pre-opening special events preparation paid off ten days after the opening on Friday, May 26, with a reading and talk by the dean of Canadian poetry, Earle Birney, sponsored by the Canada Council, that brought in 70 people. As the founder and first chairman

Earle Birney

Lloyd DeJong, Earle Birney,
Judith Copithorne, Gerry
Gilbert

of the Creative Writing department at UBC, Birney's appearance was immaculately well-timed and had the effect of bestowing an official tribal blessing on the Literary Storefront. The Friday 8 PM start time established the precedent for readings on the last Friday evening of every month.[ii] Many writers met other writers they'd admired for the first time. Cathy Ford recounts her experience:

> The first time I met Dorothy Livesay, in person, as compared to on the page, or in listening at a poetry reading, was at one of many Literary Storefront performance events . . . It was one of the occasions when Maxine Gadd and Roy Kiyooka were trying to teach me to drink Scotch, with the avowed resultant clarity of mind, no mixer and no hangover, promises. We were sitting at either end of the same sagging couch. Dorothy said she was delighted to meet me. "Oh Dorothy," I said, in my bravest alcohol-induced voice, "I am surprised. I have always been told you could be such a bear." "My dear," she said, "I am never a bear to young women poets."[63]

In the ensuing weeks, Fertig wrote a constitution, and the Literary Storefront was registered on October 5, 1979, as a non-profit called Friends of the Literary Storefront Society. Ultimately it would be the first literary group to receive provincial funding and would open the door for other literary organizations. The objects included:

a) To advance knowledge and appreciation of and to stimulate interest and development in the literary arts through workshops, courses, readings, lectures, exhibits, information services, meetings, publications, special events and otherwise.

b) To educate the general public as to the importance of the literary arts and promote interaction and support between writers and between the writer and community.

---

ii   Other readings would quickly follow with 80 people attending a Dorothy Livesay reading, then Helene Rosenthal, Betty Lambert, Ishmael Katz, Mary Beth Knechtel, David Watmough, Jack Hodgins, Florence McNeil, bill bissett, Cathy Ford, Eileen Kernaghan, Jennifer Alley, John Harding, Sheila McCarthy, Christopher Levenson and Peter Trower.

c) To provide a centre for study, meetings and events with an eventual stride towards national and international involvement and exchange.

d) To provide a focus for West Coast writers.

e) To apply for, raise and to receive grants, legacies, devices and bequests and to hold, administer, invest, expend or deal with the same in furtherance of the objects of the Society.

f) To do all such other things as are incidental or conducive to the attainment of the objects of the Society.

As Fertig wrote the Society's constitution, she had in mind the operational model of Place des Arts in Maillardville, Coquitlam, a French-Canadian bastion originally built up around the Fraser River sawmills and the home of Lucille Starr, who Sylvia Tyson calls Canada's greatest woman country singer. As Fertig reflects, "There weren't any literary centre models in Canada so I went for the only arts centre constitution I could find." She discussed the choice with her supporters. Cathy Ford, a Storefront member, endorsed her point of view:

Mona understood from the beginning that the grounding, the

Tom Wayman, Peter Haase, Dorothy Livesay, Mona Fertig

Dorothy Livesay, Roy Kiyooka

formalizing was crucial. Many bright ideas and challenges to the status quo in Vancouver had already turned into one-offs. The notion of opening a place and a space for everyone to be able to access, be welcomed and included, was entirely new and was a kind of mission statement that the Storefront celebrated—to many people's amusement and surprise. Mona's instincts were right about this; it was a joy to see people's reaction to being one of the many. We were happily all small fish meeting in the big Storefront pool. Even those of us who thought we should perhaps caution our optimism or idealism with self-protection from the egoists and shining stars were more than once shocked, delighted, rehumanzied.[64]

Patrick Lane wrote, "my congratulations on what you are doing there — perhaps it will finally break down the walls of cliques, claques and back-biting VCR is so famous for — keep up the good work — it is appreciated more than you know..."

On June 12, a month after opening, Mona wrote a request to extend her Explorations grant for a period of four months, so that her funding would be for a full year. This would provide sufficient time to get the Literary Storefront off the ground. The amount requested was $3,840.

Meantime, the fuller scope of the new centre's offerings began defining itself. Literary films were seen as a regular program event at the Storefront, and with equipment loans from the Video Inn, they commenced with *An Inquiry into the Life and Death of Malcolm Lowry*, and the National Film Board's exceptional library of literary documentaries was shown, introducing audiences to steady portraits of Canada's established author personalities. In July, courtesy of John Shinnick, a tape of Jack Kerouac reading his poetry with piano accompaniment by Steve Allen brought the visual and verbal architecture of beat poetics to Vancouver's perennial coterie of beat enthusiasts.

By the summer of 1979, Mona's idea of offering a slate of writing workshops came to fruition. She wrote to various teacher-writers she knew or had heard of and invited them to teach; often they were members of The Writers' Union or the League of Poets. The instructors were well-paid, and the workshops generated income for the Storefront. By October, the first program of titles and instructors was finalized: Short Fiction, with Audrey Thomas; Journalism, with Andreas Schroeder; The Commercial Novel, with Keith Maillard; and The Writer as Performer, led by David Watmough, Canada's foremost public literary reader who promised, "a workshop for writers of poetry, fiction or plays who wish to publically perform their work aloud. To be discussed are such intrinsic factors as audience attention, proper selection of materials, and learning to understand your own voice. Each student will be worked with individually. The sense of accomplishment that resulted flowed two ways: When Anne Marriott, who had written for decades, taught a Poetry workshop—she signed a book for Mona and inscribed, "With appreciation for the Storefront and all it's brought us." Marriott's poem "Woodyards in the Rain" remains a Vancouver classic.

The Storefront walls were eminently suitable for small print exhibitions, and Mona organized various displays. The first included Talonbooks author posters and Pulp Press broadsheets and book posters. Later came an exhibit of *Boxed Words* by Beth Jankola, *Writers' Rejection Letters*, Carole Itter's *Alphabet* and paintings by bill bissett.

A notice board provided info about readings around town and posted events or announcements. From the outset, the Storefront's monthly newsletter also featured contributions of poetry and work by John Pass, Cathy Ford, Eileen Kernaghan and Hope Andersen. As the summer progressed and audiences came and returned for more, the list of readers grew commensurately.[iii]

With their Co-op Radio experience and Peter's background as a musician, Fertig and Haase taped most of the headliner readings, cre-

---

iii   Anne Cameron, P.K. Page, Susan Musgrave, Marilyn Bowering, Robert Harlow, Scott Lawrance, Mark Warrior, Tom Wayman, Greg Gatenby, Joanne Yamaguchi, Avron Hoffman, Kevin Roberts and Carolyn Zonailo all made the trek.

ating a wealth of over one hundred and twenty-five sound recordings while she was the director.[65]

Evelyn Fertig, who was a volunteer receptionist at CFRO, knew Ingrid Klassen, who was also a volunteer at CFRO. Klassen became aware of Evelyn as a very psychic woman. Klassen, who also knew Beth Jankola, attended a reading with Evelyn and decided to "get involved with the energy" at the Storefront. She found Mona Fertig as bright a spirit as her mother:

Mona treated everyone equally, had respect for everyone; that was her great quality. She didn't have a hierarchy of people that she respected. And she had people skills. She knew how to be supportive and nurturing to writers. It was part of her mission statement to herself.[66]

Other good things continued to unfold. On September 26, 1978, the

Glenn Pearson, Craig
Spence, Pasquale Pascucci

extension of the Explorations grant was received. Emerging writer
Craig Spence, who joined the newsletter editorial group in October,
remembers:

The Literary Storefront nurtured and challenged me as a poet
and writer during a pivotal point in my life. At the time I had no
confidence in my abilities and didn't know where to begin. To be
around poets and writers in an environment where it was okay to
experiment helped me in ways I don't think I have fully appreciated
to this day. It was a place where I could go and be special even though
I wasn't accomplished or ready as a writer. I think people there recognized that the purpose was to support the will to write—which
can so easily be crushed—as much as the actual writing. I have tried
joining writer's groups since, but have never found a replacement for
the Literary Storefront."[67]

By November 1978, Fertig was able to announce that more than

Clockwise from top left:
Mona Fertig, Marilyn Bowering, Susan Musgrave
Scott Lawrance, Robert Harlow
Harvey Chometsky
Mark Warrior

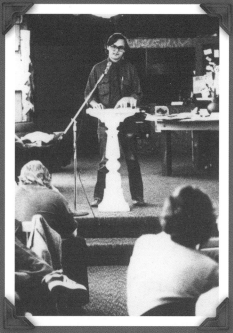

Clockwise from top left: Beth Jankola; Hope Anderson; Joanne Yamaguchi, Avron Hoffman; Unknown reader; Tom Wayman, Gwen Hauser

3,000 people had visited the Storefront or attended events there. By the following month, more than 120 memberships had been sold. Group members included the Surrey Art Gallery, Periodical Writers Association of Canada (PWAC), St. George's School, the Burnaby Writers' Society, and The Writers' Union of Canada (TWUC). Publisher Scott McIntyre of Douglas & McIntyre wrote, "It took too long but I finally made it in. An application form and cheque for becoming a member will follow."

Throughout the new space, décor was bohemian chic, with the lending library, filing cabinet, plants, couches, coffee table, podium,[68] desk, chairs, a rack of literary magazines and a large round table that Peter had built for workshops. "The Literary Storefront's comfortable atmosphere (and furniture), along with its library and coffee pot, served as a sort of living room for Vancouver writers—a place to relax, rendezvous with others of the literary persuasion."[69] Large laminated *Shakespeare & Company* photos of Ezra Pound, Djuna Barnes, T.S. Eliot, Janet Flanner, Ernest Hemingway, James Joyce and Sylvia Beach, and Hilda Doolittle hung on the wall. As the months progressed, new framed black-and-white photos of Storefront readers would gradually appear on the wall, adding contemporary faces to the legends. There were empty change rooms from the Storefront's original incarnation that stood empty but gave people cause for laughter from time to time. The back third of the Storefront was raised a level higher than the front. This gave the semblance of a stage, which made for more effective group dynamics during readings. The office, which sat against the back wall with its big open window, doubled as a bar at night. The floors were industrial carpeted and the ceilings high. Logistically, there were a few awkward necessities: the washroom was outside and down the stairs, so during events people had to use a key. On Water Street, the refurbished square had been locked by nightfall; for evening events, the gates had to be unlocked, and people were directed to come up through a side gate; it could get complicated. With the rest of the businesses in the square shut and dark, the Storefront could seem almost like a beacon—a light in the night.

The principles Fertig had founded the Storefront upon were its initial draw, but negotiating your way into the Storefront space and community could still take some stick-handling. "The Storefront wasn't cliquey, but it could be intimidating," long-time member ElJean Wilson reflects. "I was still working on my early writing at the time and felt a bit of an outsider."[70] Memberships were open to everyone, however, and at $12 a year, it included receiving a monthly newsletter full of information, use of the lending library that eventually had over 2,000 titles (many of them signed), use of the Storefront for meetings and in-store use of typewriters.

Running successful literary events requires solid organizing skills, common-sense business expertise and gumption. Fertig had enough energy and courage to compensate for raw expertise and had been organizing readings and events for six years. Her experience at the Surrey Art Gallery was also an asset as it had been an ideal training opportunity in the type of administration the Literary Storefront required. Time and labour were necessary to ensure that obligations regarding publicity, hospitality, minding the door and selling books were properly attended to. Initially Fertig coordinated all of this and had volunteers set up and host the open readings each month. The volunteers were entrusted with the keys and carried on in the shared spirit of optimism. Evening events typically were scheduled for 8 PM, with doors open half an hour before show times to allow for informal mixing and browsing the steadily expanding shelves of donated books and magazines. Later, to assist in selling tickets, Fertig made arrangements with Duthie Books on Robson Street, Richard Pender Books on Pender Street and Octopus Books in Kitsilano and East Vancouver.

Open readings were now an enduring feature of Storefront activity and ran on Sunday evenings, once a month, from 7 to 9 PM. Readers

John Warren, Peter Haase
at bar. P.K. Page art in
background

Alex Wayman

were invited to bring their poetry, fiction, translations or various
other forms of works in progress that, in a broad sense, encompassed
song, monologue, portions of scripts for stage or television, work for
multiple voices and so on. Readings were approximately ten minutes
each, followed by an informal one-hour feedback session, and readers
and Storefront members were always encouraged to bring friends to
help build the audience and add to the conviviality.

Mona loved her new self-employment.

Every morning when I went to work, I would drive in from East
Van where Peter and I now lived, park my car in Japantown, and
walk to work. I loved walking through the [then] quiet and empty
city streets, in all seasons, past the Japanese shops, the galleries, the
Sunrise market, the reflecting hotel windows, to open the Storefront.
There would often be a poet or a budding writer waiting outside to
come in. I loved the excitement of those days. Roy Kiyooka ran his
photography gallery The Blue Mule on Powell Street, and I would
sometimes stop by on my way home.[71]

The *Province* reported on May 12, 1978, that The Writers' Union

of Canada had agreed in principle to set up its first regional office in Vancouver for a trial period of three months.[72] This followed sustained lobbying by its B.C. members—the largest regional membership outside of Ontario at the time—including novelists David Watmough, Keith Maillard, Audrey Thomas, Andreas Schroeder, Sandy Frances Duncan and Robert Harlow. Following a unanimous decision at its national AGM in Ottawa, when its chair was the redoubtable social justice activist and journalist June Callwood, the BC Branch took up office at the Storefront by October at Fertig's invitation. Regular business hours were Tuesday and Thursday, 1:30 to 5:30 PM when a TWUC member sat at the desk and provided information regarding book contracts, copyright and publishing to all who walked in. They offered a manuscript evaluation service, a special Writers in the Schools

Pasquale Pascucci, Storefront member, Peter Haase on Halloween

program and readings for their members. David Watmough was the B.C. Rep, and Vancouver writer Joan Haggerty became their first member to look after the desk. She recalls:

I used to sit at the desk at the front and wait for people to come in who wanted to talk about writing. They did too. I particularly remember Bill Deverell coming into the Storefront with his first-ever manuscript and asking me how he should go about finding a publisher, where he should send his first unpublished novel, and whether he should get a professional reading first, etc. I remember his visit vividly; we sat over on the couch. I was thrilled when he later succeeded so impressively.[73]

William Deverell had his Deverell, Harrop and Co. law office in Gastown at Gaolers Mews, in the former Alhambra Hotel, overlooking

Joan Haggerty of The Writers' Union

Maple Tree Square a few steps away. He observes:

There's a history [to that book], yes, and it involved my law partner, now Madam Justice Nancy Morrison and Judy LaMarsh, a former Liberal cabinet minister who gave my manuscript directly to Jack McClelland . . . I immediately joined TWUC on getting published and went to my first AGM in Ontario.[74]

TWUC's ancillary literary operation amplified the reach and calibre of literary service the evolving Storefront "centre" had to offer. It meant that serious working writers would be dropping by, and others on the way up or looking in had a chance to rub shoulders with them and soak up a little more literary ambience. Life at the Storefront now had a little more professional shine. Up the road at the downtown public library, staff began referring people with routine queries about writing and publishing to the Storefront and The Writers' Union office.

Audrey Thomas

4

1979: Patterns of Order,
Day-to-day Operations

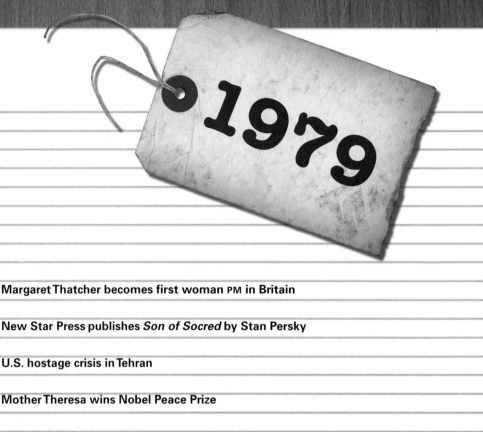

1979

Margaret Thatcher becomes first woman PM in Britain

New Star Press publishes *Son of Socred* by Stan Persky

U.S. hostage crisis in Tehran

Mother Theresa wins Nobel Peace Prize

Three Mile Island nuclear reactor disaster

Soviet Union invades Afghanistan

Leftist Sandinistas take over in Nicaragua as dictator Somoza flees

Granville Island Market opens

Francis Ford Coppola's *Apocalypse Now* stuns with its depiction of Vietnam War

China implements one-child policy

Raincoast Books established

Alice Munro is writer-in-residence at UBC

January 1979 opened with *Boxed Words*, a literary mixed-media exhibition by Fertig's mentor, Beth Jankola. A narrative poet of the Vancouver School, as George Woodcock, the city's éminence gris man of letters, had it, Jankola's "verbal dexterity . . . often dips and deepens below the imagist epidermis" (*Beat*, Jankola, 1994). In March, Al Neil and Carole Itter continued the Vancouver line with their reading. Itter had worked with poet Daphne Marlatt for two years on the Strathcona Heritage project, and Neil would read from his beat noir novel *Slammer*.

In January, Audrey Thomas also read from her new novel, *Latakia*, and Robin Skelton, the celebrated poet-witch and chair of the University of Victoria's Department of Creative Writing, read in February.[75] Skelton was surprised at being invited to read and explained to Fertig that not many Vancouver writers were interested in his work. Even within the B.C. writing community, there appeared to be Vancouver and Victoria solitudes. He stayed at Peter and Mona's on Joyce Road, where Peter cooked a curry dinner and they talked for hours. Few turned up for his reading, as Robin had rightly projected, but the occasion helped develop a useful link between the Storefront and Vancouver Island writers, among whom Skelton was a spark-plug personality.

Boxed Words

Al Neil, Trevor Carolan at Equinox Gallery
Photograph by Kwangshik Kwon

THE LITERARY STOREFRONT NEWSLETTER NOVEMBER no. 6

35¢

no.7

35¢

GIRL BATTLES WITH TYPEWRITER

The Literary Storefront Newsletter

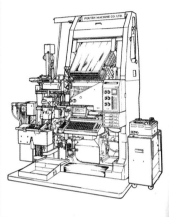

The **Literary Storefront Newsletter**

Number 9   February 1979

APRIL

35¢

the Literary Storefront Newsletter

No 11

THE Literary storefront NEWSLETTER

35¢

may 79

no. 12

Literary Storefront Newsletter

May '81

50 cents

The Newsletter

One of the most essential communication tools of the Literary Storefront enterprise was the monthly newsletter. Published from June 1978 onward, its circulation rose to 500 copies. From the outset, Mona was the general editor with many contributors in support. Quick-printed with a different coloured cover for each edition, at the cost of $80 a month it brought readers news of upcoming literary events, of who had published what and where, of educational opportunities and of miscellaneous items from around B.C.'s general arts and publishing world. As Jean Mallinson recalls, "The newsletter was a hands-on production in every way. I remember rainy afternoons spent with Mona, her mother Evelyn and other volunteers, putting the pages of the Storefront newsletter together."[76]

Modest by the standards of today's computer-produced publicity, the newsletter, with pull-out calendar, also published information on markets, editing services and literary periodicals; printed reviews of new books of poetry and fiction; announced writing workshops; and published poems. Remarkably, it kept its focus intensely local. Occasionally reports might percolate through of a member's attendance at a festival or conference back east or in the U.S., but mainly the information was Vancouver-based, with updates from Victoria, Nanaimo and, from time to time, the Kootenays and Okanagan. A scan through the newsletter's monthly event listings would show readers and dates for events at Douglas College in Surrey and New Westminster, UBC, Simon Fraser University, Capilano College, Malaspina College in Nanaimo and Camosun College and the University of Victoria in the island capital. Bookstore and public library reading events were announced, as were literary gatherings planned by others elsewhere in Vancouver.

Whether new or professionally affiliated, there was nothing else like it for writers. Professional national organizations such as The

Writers' Union, the League of Canadian Poets, Alliance of Canadian Cinema Television and Radio Artists (ACTRA), the Periodical Writers Association of Canada or the long-standing Canadian Authors Association made information available to their members, but this obliged membership fees that younger writers often could not afford, or applications subject to "professional" publication history, public reading experience or academic teaching or editing work, which many did not have. For these, apart from event listings in the daily newspapers and the *Georgia Straight,* the notice boards at the public library or in bookstores were the usual way of keeping track of what was going on. No email or social networking buzz existed then. The Storefront newsletter was an affordable, timely and vital addition to communication within the city's non-academic, non-professionally affiliated writers. It also opened access to other downtown and regionally isolated but practising writers and artists, and academics, crossing all boundaries, all ways. If it was unevenly produced and typeset, with cover art that ranged from doodles to a variety of drawings and images, its mimeographed, 8½" x 11" folded and stapled booklet format of usually 16 pages was followed with keen interest nonetheless. It sold at first for 25 cents then quickly rose to 35 cents. Compared to the newsletter of the Poetry Project in NYC, which was a simple plain newsletter copied on 8½" x 11" and stapled in the corner, it was a livelier, better-designed Canadian model.[iv] By April 1979 (issue #11), Peter Goodchild was listed as poetry editor and Pasquale Pascucci as open reading host. In a kind of literary

---

iv   Contributors to the newsletter's editorial and graphic production included Louise T. Gallant, Cathy Ford, Carolyn Zonailo, Hannah Skapski, Eileen Kernaghan, Peter Goodchild, Maggi Shore, Craig Spence, Glen Pearson, John Pass, Opal L. Nations, Heather Haley, Hope Anderson, Tom Wayman, Joan Bellinger, Robin Ridington, Sylvie-Anne Delalune, Jonie Anderson, R.A. Kawalilak, Pat Robertson, Nellie McClung, Mike Constable, K.O. Kanne, Helen Potrebenko and book reviewer Alan Twigg, "alive and well and freelancing his way to fame and fortune." Graphic art was provided by bill bissett, Beth Jankola, Tim Lander, Peter Haase, Ed Varney, Maggi Shore and Trevor McKeown who was "looking for work."

ecumenism, the Literary Storefront newsletter also began a tradition of dedicating specific editions in memory of great poets and writers of various genres. The July 1978 edition (#2) was dedicated to Louis Zukofsky (January 23, 1904–May 12, 1978). Other occasional tribute editions would follow.

Peter Haase thinks back to that time:

I was involved a lot with the newsletter from the beginning. A little bit with design, illustration and the covers. We were then living on Joyce Road near Kingsway in East Vancouver, and Mona used to get home late at night, dog-tired, but straightaway she'd be on the phone organizing more readings, gathering paperwork. She worked day and night.[77]

Canada Council start-up funding extended until May 1979. Subsequent to this, funding would remain a constant challenge. Membership came in several levels—with brick $16, membership with T-shirt $16, group membership $20, group with brick $25, newsletter only $6. Readings, workshops and special events added to the ledger sheet, but the Storefront program was still a work in progress. The newsletter urged readers to submit fundraising ideas, and the gamut of offerings ranged widely. If most of the ideas came from Mona and Peter, the fundraising submissions brainstormed with a few dedicated members were understandably often tied to literary genres or organizational interests, and these brought a variety and freshness to the Storefront's events unlike others in town.

Literary Storefront T-shirts seemed a good promotional idea and sold for $6. Mail orders were a bargain 50 cents extra. Men's shirts came in large and medium, dark blue and dark green; women's shirts were medium or small, dark red or yellow.

Music events have always been a signature badge of Vancouver's countercultural otherness. For a number of writers who performed in bands and folk groups, the Storefront's downtown location in funky

Peter and Mona
Photograph by
Milton Bingham

Gastown made it a desirable site. Alan Twigg performed there, as well as local Celtic fiddlers. Robert Priest, the Toronto poet, would drop by and play his guitar and sing on the old couch when he was out west on reading tours. Music collaborations would remain a part of the centre's ethos connecting its purely literary nature with Fertig's original Storefront idea that included a salon or poetry bookshop-communal party nexus component. By the next year, Peter Trower and Susie Whiten would also be performing for Storefront audiences.

The *Birthday Book* anthology of contributions from members or supporters was a special project initiative. Not all the Storefront's key volunteers were established literary people; in fact most were not. Many were emerging writers who took a while to feel confident about their work, or were still finding their way with words and attended the Storefront's open readings. For those still unsure of their vocation or wary of venturing among the literary police, these open events were important as a channel into the literary world and a safe environment in which to test the waters, to meet others in the same situation or to meet writers they might have heard of through the newspaper or from the radio. It was a rare opportunity to grow, slow and unwatched, but supported. Nor were all regular attendees at Storefront events writers themselves. Many modest, committed audience members came to listen and learn from the presence of real, living writers whose work they admired. For those aiming to publish, the *Birthday Book,* to celebrate the Storefront's first year of operation, was a gate of opportunity. The limited edition of 200 copies sold for $1.50, with 40 cents added for mailing. Who wouldn't want to be published? It was edited by Peter Goodchild, a quiet, observant writer who was drawn to the Storefront by Fertig's pre-publicity and became one of its first volunteers. In recognition of a job well done and with soul, Beth Jankola wrote Goodchild a postcard saying, "Looks like your head isn't always in the clouds Peter—you're a good editor!"[v]

The Storefront was a natural outlet for selling local books and regional literary magazines. In the spring of 1979, it began selling books on consignment, with none priced more than $5. Authors dropped off four copies of each title at a time with the selling price marked on them. The Storefront took the customary bookstore share of 40

---

v   The *Birthday Book* featured work by a roster of excellent contributors, veterans and newer writers including Peter Christensen, Dorothy Livesay, Sylvie-Anne Delalune, Barry Dempster, Tom Wayman, Daphne Marlatt, Cathy Ford, Deborah Foulks, Elizabeth Gourlay, Eldon Grier, Beth Jankola, R.A. Kawalilak, Sarah-Marie Loupe, Dorothy Manning, Phil Menger, Anne Miles, Morgan Nyberg, Pasquale Pascucci, Helen Potrebenko, Philip Quinn, Dennis Reid, Patricia Robertson, Helene Rosenthal, L. Santosha, Liza Smaller, Craig Spence, Lorraine Vernon, G.P. Walsh, Joanne Yamaguchi, Avron Hoffman, Jennifer Alley, Carolyn Zonailo and Mona Fertig.

Peter Goodchild

Avron Hoffman and
Joanne Yamaguchi

percent from the top and mailed cheques when all copies had sold. The low prices and the operation's size meant that financially it would always be a modest proposition, yet the operation and distribution space for writers and publishers meant there was at least one outlet for a writer's books in Vancouver. Any writer who had had to bear up to the challenge of porting her or his own books around the city and trying to place them in bookshops knew the psychological value of having at least one reliable outlet. For first-time or self-published writers, this meant a lot. Literary magazines such as *Gut*, *Grain*, *Room of One's Own*, *Capilano Review*, *Canadian Literature*, *acanthus* and *Prism International* were also sold.

Dennis Reid and friend

First *Birthday Book*

A zanier idea was the campaign that asked Storefront supporters to donate their notorious five "free BRIC shares" in the British Columbia Resource Investment Corporation. The Social Credit government had given these away in 1979 as an experiment in what *BC Business* magazine termed "citizen capitalism." Each five-share dole was worth $30, and for a time, they traded hands before becoming a collector's item, although worthless. Perhaps an idea ahead of its time, no records indicate how much (or how little) the net was from this initiative—a harbinger of modern arts fundraising strategies that solicit air miles and securities from supporters.

Borrowing a page from academic summer conferences in Vancouver that traditionally featured a harbour tour among their supplementary attractions, a five-hour Benefit Fundraising Cruise deep into Indian Arm, past Malcolm Lowry's old squatter territory just beyond the Ironworkers Memorial Second Narrows Bridge, was advertised for Sunday, July 30. The $20 (BYOB) tariff included music, food and ice, with departure from near Port Moody. Hopes were high regarding erotic literary possibilities aboard the seventy-three-foot charter vessel, perhaps fittingly called the Promiscuity, then cancelled by low registration.

The Storefront also began advertising its space for rent for meetings or literary and cultural events, at a $30 fee. This helped to make the premises a useful adjunct space for other local literary organizations that needed a site for their seminars, teaching events, monthly or annual general meetings and so on. In the late 1970s, rental space for arts groups in Vancouver was in chronic short supply and frequently at a prohibitive cost. The opportunity to welcome one's own organizational members to a learning event was a valuable asset, particularly because it introduced them to an already functioning literary space that many had not previously known of. The Writers' Union of Canada negotiated rental of an office space from the Storefront for $120 per month that included phone service.

Stiff news came in April 1979: Vancouver's City Council under conservative Mayor Jack Volrich rejected the Storefront's application for organizational cultural assistance. Under the previous, more arts-sympathetic mayor, Art Phillips, it might have been a different outcome, but he had left municipal politics to enter Canada's federal parliament as a Liberal. Fertig had been hoping for encouraging news, and the rejection came as a blow. The end of that same month marked the Storefront's first fateful year of existence, and Fertig published a brief note in the newsletter:

An attendance [at Storefront events over one year] of 7,000 and a membership of almost 200 says more than any lengthy synopsis. This close also brings us to the end of the Canada Council Explorations grant, which paid for rent and a small salary for the Director. At the beginning of May [1979] we enter into our second year on a very low budget relying mainly on memberships, course and workshop registrations and donations. Rental of small office space will also be available to interested literary groups or individuals. The Literary Storefront as a nerve centre void of any narrow political vision welcomes all ideas and input. The initial dream/idea has only strengthened.[78]

Fertig was already mindful of the weather ahead. By May 1979, the Storefront's Explorations grant support would conclude. Nevertheless, in a gesture supportive of struggling members, Writers On Welfare programs were made available through Vancouver's municipal Community Involvement Program and Incentive Allowance for Employment Preparation. Compensation was $50, paid by the City for twenty hours of work each month. Lorene de Courcy, Renee Rodin and G.P. Walsh as well as five others joined the program. They catalogued donated books, looked after memberships and worked on the newsletter. The people who applied for the program were writers, poets, journalists, single mothers, people who had worked for the CBC and the like. Renee Rodin recalls:

Coming from Montreal and being a writer myself, I was hungry for literary life. As a single mother on welfare, I was eligible to earn a little extra money if it were at an "approved" place. Mona was gracious enough to hire me to come in a couple of afternoons a week to help with the massive paperwork involved in running the Storefront. It felt great to be at such an exciting hub devoted entirely to literature and where you never knew which writers were going to drop by. But it was the evening readings that really stood out for me.[79]

The year's real news was in the Storefront's obtaining non-profit society and also federal charitable status. It could now issue tax receipts. The newsletter was able to announce a first anonymous patron, whom Fertig suggests was probably Jane Rule. There were others who anonymously contributed to the newsletter production by paying for printing or postage.

The Workshops

The Storefront's literary workshop programs soon expanded. The slate of offerings grew in scope and featured songwriters, a storytelling workshop for children with Jane Munro and feminist events such as a Creation Myths series. Andreas Schroeder offered a first professional development workshop called Writing Fiction, followed by a series lined up for the early fall with Governor General's Award winner Anne Marriott leading a Poetry and Children session, and Alan Oman teaching Television Drama Writing—previously a fortress of privileged knowledge gained only through very expensive weekend workshops. A democratization of literary information had begun.

The roster of workshops would further evolve to include The Process of Poetry, with Cathy Ford; Writing for Radio, with Phil Menger; and Canadian Writing in the 1930's, with Dorothy Livesay. Livesay's topics would address writing prose documentaries, "Agit Prop" plays, mass chants, poetry and its influences, and fiction (especially *Waste Heritage* by Irene Baird). Writing for Children would feature discussion nights and evening workshops with Anne Blades, Sue Ann Alderson, Norma Charles, Christie Harris, Sandy Frances Duncan and Doug Tait. Ferron would lead a session on Songwriting.

The workshops, designed for groups of eight to fifteen participants, did well, attracting registrations with the promise of close personal access to respected authors and artists with deep experience. By year's end, the accounts showed substantial revenues of $4,583.25 from enrolments. These literary workshops were successful and filled a need for non-academic access to skills and jobs-oriented training, or professional renewal. They were also the forerunner of the downtown SFU Centre for Studies in Publishing and Writing that would open decades later, just a few blocks away on Hastings Street.

Jack Hodgins, another instructor recruited by Fertig, recalls:

An invitation to conduct a workshop at the Literary Storefront in Vancouver came at a time when I had been teaching high-school for many years but had little experience conducting workshops with adult writers. An opportunity for this small-town Islander to work with Vancouver writers, though intimidating, was irresistible. I remember a very informal set-up where we sat on comfortable couches and armchairs to talk about writing. This took place in a large upper storey room where we were surrounded by books and the office-like equipment for some mysterious business overseen by Mona and her mother, two rather exotic women of considerable energy and imagination. I'm sure the workshops were far less planned or structured than I later developed, but the opportunity to work with Vancouver writers I may not have met otherwise gave me the confidence to attend Writers' Union meetings on the mainland in the following years. For me, the Literary Storefront was a welcome doorway to the world of Big City writers.[80]

Events sparkled when Roy Kiyooka headed a much-talked-about Year of the Goat reading, and a set of eighteen of his offset prints from *The Fontainebleau Dream Machine*, published by Coach House Press, was the door prize.[vi] At another creatively engaged event, Daphne Marlatt read with Toronto's Penn Kemp for the first time and remembers "how electrifying it was to hear a woman play the pitches of her own voice and language acuity, to recognize that the terrain the Four Horsemen or Owen Sound were exploring could also be a terrain for a woman's voice to explore."[81]

---

vi   Spring readings featured Gerry Gilbert, Dale Zieroth, Matt Cohen, Jane Munro, Elizabeth Gourlay, Eldon Grier, Rosalind MacPhee, Naomi Rachel, Peter Christensen, George McWhirter, Ann West, Paul Gotro, Carolyn Zonailo, Marya Fiamengo, Karl Siegler, Reschard Gool, Myra McFarlane, Rona Murray and David McFadden.

Fertig remained notably supportive of women writers and of creating a space for their voices to be heard. This was an important factor for many emerging and established women writers, and they stated it over and over years later.

March 22 saw an important launch party for *D'Sonoqua*, a path-breaking two-volume anthology of thirty-two British Columbia women poets, edited by Ingrid Klassen and published by Intermedia Press. It contained work by Carolyn Borsman, Marilyn Bowering, G.V.

Jack Hodgins and fan

Daphne Marlatt,
Penn Kemp

Downes, Marya Fiamengo, Elizabeth Gourlay, Rosemary Hollings-
head, Stephanie Judy, Pat Lowther, Myra MacFarlane, Floris McLaren,
Florence McNeil, Dorothy Manning, Daphne Marlatt, Judi Morton,
Rona Murray, Helene Rosenthal, Roslyn Smythe and Phyllis Webb.[vii]
Alan Twigg reviewed the collection favourably in the newsletter,
noting the strength of known poets like Florence McNeil.

Poet and artist Rhoda Rosenfeld confirmed the significance of such
events at the Literary Storefront, observing, "The Literary Storefront
kept us alive for poetry during the late '70s, early '80s. Mona's gen-
erosity, warmth and commitment created a space where literature,
especially women's writing, was able to live."[82]

Poet and critic Jean Mallinson looks back on it all with affection:

It was a romantic venture but it was also pragmatic. Just walk
up those long stairs, open the door, and you would be part of it . . .
I remember above all the feeling of being where literature was hap-

---

vii   Featured contributors also included Judith Copithorne, Mona Fertig, Cathy Ford, Maxine
Gadd, Leona Gom, Carole Itter, Beth Jankola, Nellie McClung, Anne Marriott, Susan Musgrave,
Marguerite Pinney, Dona Sturmanis, Lorraine Vernon, Carolyn Zonailo.

D'Sonoqua book launch

pening, where poetry was what mattered . . . Changed as we may be, we are still living on the energies of that time.[83]

Carole Itter's collaborative reading with Al Neil is still remembered by Storefront veterans. Itter recollects:

I recall a fair amount of planning on my part and also being quite nervous to be working with someone as illustrious as Al Neil—I think it was the first time we had done something together. In the performance part, I had a huge white linen tablecloth wrapped around hundreds of glass shards that I had collected from the beach at Dollarton and I spilled them, all in one motion, across the floor [of the stage]. Quite a good sound. He and I alternated voices, reading a piece I had written about bringing a third person into a marriage bed. I wrote the piece twice, switching genders, and the emotions seemed to be somewhat the same. We read it in tandem.[84]

The Storefront's April newsletter added an extra dimension when

Alan Twigg contributed reviews of books by selected local authors. A widely published literary journalist who would go on to publish *BC BookWorld* and author many books, Twigg provided insights into new work when reviews for B.C. writers were not as common as they would become. His thoughts on Carolyn Zonailo's *Zone 5*, Morgan Nyberg's *Crazy Horse Suite* and Betty Lambert's *Crossings* were perceptive reviews, unafraid to express an opinion.

In April, the Canada Council awarded the Literary Storefront a book kit of 200 titles from its Book Donation Competition.[viii] Shepherded by Gerry Walsh and Rhoda Rosenfeld, the Storefront's library was growing and becoming a formidable resource for Canadian literature. Mona taught volunteers how to catalogue books using the Dewey Decimal System, and a card filing box was set up. Storefront library borrowing privileges made another good reason to join up or renew one's membership.

May brought an offbeat special event to the literary community, the *Rejection Letter Display*. "Felt rejected lately? Don't use those letters for wallpaper," the public call exclaimed. "We need them for our display. Pick out the meanest, funniest, nicest, longest, and shortest, and send them (or good photocopies) on to us." It was duly mounted.

The Birthday Benefit bash on May 12, celebrating the Storefront's first year, was rocking forward. For the night, two vacant stores next to the Storefront would be opened up for a large dance area. Food and refreshments were sold, door prizes given away, photographs of the past year's events displayed and a graffiti wall marked by wannabe artists and memoirists. There was birthday cake at midnight, the new *Birthday Book* anthology and T-shirts for sale, and open-mic readings that were sure to help swell the crowd. Not a bad deal for $3.

---

viii   This comprised the likes of Northrop Frye, George Woodcock, Margaret Atwood, Jane Rule, Emily Carr, Jean-Guy Carrier, Susan Musgrave, Jack Hodgins, Margaret Mitchell, John Newlove, Max Braithwaite, Ken Mitchell, James Reaney, Patrick Watson, Hugh Hood, Michel Tremblay, among many others.

The ensuing summer and fall brought a raft of news, reading events and the Storefront's first fundraising book sale. Newsletter announcements mentioned the Naropa Institute's summer writing program, which perennial Vancouver favourite Allen Ginsberg had started with Anne Waldman. The Buddhist school's catalogue of courses, progressing as the Jack Kerouac School of Disembodied Poetics at Naropa's Boulder, Colorado campus and its promotional catalogue were available at the Storefront. For an up-and-coming writer like Richard Olafson, who would go on to publish regularly as a poet and also become an enduring regional literary publisher with Ekstasis Editions, or a tribal elder in search of new horizons such as Bob Hunter, the city's pioneering gonzo journalist and Greenpeace flagman, word of Naropa's hip programs wafted through like a breeze of internationalism, of possibility. Remarkably, such news also helped make accreditation possible for B.C. students to attend courses at Naropa on their student loans. Arts administrators were following the Storefront newsletter, as were hustling freelancers like me.

Around town, local lawyer William Deverell won the Seal Books First Novel Award of $50,000 for his gripping Chinatown novel *Needles*, which he'd made inquiries about at the Storefront. Another name in the news was prominent novelist and gender rights activist Jane Rule. She added her weight to the Storefront's teaching reputation by agreeing to lead a day-long Sunday workshop in October titled Questions for Gay Writers. Participants were asked to bring up to 500 words on this subject. Rule had joined the Storefront when it first opened and remained a good supporter of Fertig's endeavours.

By now the Literary Storefront's reputation for inclusion, diversity and welcoming of eclectic talents had grown. It was the kind of renown that could occasionally trade both ways, and the different types of people who sailed in were diverse indeed. Meandering tourists formed part of the cast. However, the writers that were drawn came in every flavour: emerging, still in the closet, crazy, famous, shy, old, singing, sad, young, fat, thin, gay and retired. In the wind and rain, the sun or gloomy shade, they turned up, mostly white but now and again with some variation of colour. As a matter of record, and being a street-front centre, there were problems from time to time with writers contending with mental health issues, and on at least one occasion, Fertig had to depart urgently for safety while one troubled member raved and ranted at her in anger. He hadn't taken his medication for schizophrenia.

Meanwhile, the arc of literary life beamed on. Up the road at the East End's labour-oriented Fisherman's Hall, Utah Phillips and Friends turned up to sing music of the Industrial Workers of the World with poetry by Mark Warrior and Tom Wayman. The Storefront cheerfully sold $2 tickets for the show and helped spread news of the upcoming, much-awaited reading by Charles Bukowski at the Viking Hall on East Hastings. The latter would prove memorable for many of the 650 who attended, but disappointing to others exacerbated by a woeful number of Bukowski wannabes intent on showing their colours to the sell-out crowd. Twenty-five years later, *There's Gonna Be a God Damn Riot in Here!*, a film of Bukowski's performance that evening by Dennis Del Torre, would surface.

In organizing Storefront readings, Mona liked to feature a pair of connected writers or a theme. One famous duo was Al Purdy (*Being Alive*) and Peter Trower (*Ragged Horizons*); both packed hardrock reputations and had a passion for poetry. Mona knew they would make an excellent combo. Purdy was a huge colloquial worker poet with a voice to wake the dead, a beer-drinker, rough and ready, with an edgy nature occasionally near to belligerence—some, like Patrick Lane, called him the authentic voice of Canuck poetry. Trower was a unique poetic force in the West Coast literary community, a denizen of Vancouver's seediest bars for decades during his wildcat years as a logger. Non-academic but from brainy stock, unpretentious and

Tom Wayman and unknown
Peter Trower, unknown and Al Purdy
Al Purdy, George Bowering, Peter Trower

with political affiliations of unknown origin, Trower was a throw-back original. Canny and compassionate to younger writers who were starting out, he was a lodestar in still-nationalist CanLit times to those who believed in literature and poetry, period. And he knew how to whisper the blues in his craggy voice. If Gastown had a soul, you could likely find it sitting beside Trower in the Lamplighter Pub on Water Street a block from the Storefront, or the Railway Club where k.d. lang would get her big break.

When Trower received the invitation, he was over the moon. It was his first time reading with Al, his hero, who had once worked in a mattress factory only eight or nine blocks north of Gastown, days that he later recounted in *Piling Blood*.[85] The place was packed to the door.

The reading season's fulsome slate of poets and authors would include a steady diet of Canada Council-sponsored presenters, among them a Work Poetry night with Carolyn Borsman (commercial fishing); Kirsten Emmott, a local physician (medicine); and Howard White, the founder of Harbour Publishing and Raincoast Chronicles journal (bush work). From Montreal, Endre Farkas, poet and editor at Véhicule Press, teamed up with perennial Storefront hero Ed Varney, who dusted off his Intermedia Press credentials to read with a slide show. There was a Long Poems workshop featuring poet Carolyn Zonailo and her new collection *Split Rock*, and poet and filmmaker Colin Browne, who had recently completed a thirty-minute film entitled *Strathyre*. A week later, two other films ran: *Wood Mountain*, featuring poems by Saskatchewan's Andy Suknaski, and *First Lady of Manawaka*, a study of Margaret Laurence. As well, first novelist Britt Hagarty, with his edgy *The Prisoner of Desire*, joined Florence McNeil, Reschard Gool and Helen Potrebenko (*Taxi!*) for a publication party. Others included: Norbert Ruebesaat and Mark Mealing, the celebrated Scottish poet Liz Lochead, Daniel Halpern from New York City, Morgan Nyberg, Rose-Marie Tremblay, Robert Tyhurst,

Chris Glynn and Sally Cole. Somehow, the Storefront's gallimaufry of readers, events and themes, as well as the felicitous timing that could occur between a reading date at the Water Street location and a sudden invitation to appear on a CBC chat program, kept alive the sense that something was happening here that still felt new. Fertig was committed to keeping a tangible record of the new as well, and her dedication and compassionate attitude was appreciated by those drawn to the Storefront:

Documentation was extremely important—photography, taping readings, archiving letters, logging our library collection, the guest book... Part of it was to keep track of the numbers, of course; but another aspect was much deeper. It was historical, we were documenting something that was unique and I had a feeling it was important to retain evidence of the dream.[86]

In keeping with Mona's consistent support of women writers, there was Four Women Reading with Conni Tricys, Pat Armstrong, Judi Smith and Irene Mock, then a Six Women Reading program in the summer with Leona Gom, Beth Jankola, Gladys Hindmarch, Conni Tricys, Sharon Thesen and Rosemary Hollingshead.

Sharon Thesen writes, "When I think of the Storefront I think of Gastown and the smell of patchouli and dope (a great fragrance combo I miss!) and a great caring for poetry. It was where I did my first reading."[87]

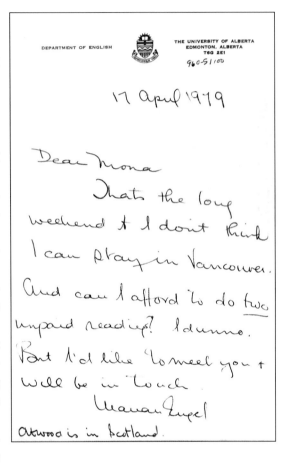

Letter from Marian Engel

Carole Itter,
Liz Lochhead

A brace of what the French like to call manifestations also took place. In late June, the San Francisco Bay Area eco-feminist Charlene Spretnak appeared. She was involved in researching and poetically reclaiming the myths of the earliest known deities of the Mediterranean world—the pre-Olympian goddesses. It was very much of the feminist spiritual odyssey of the times, and idealistically attuned with Vancouver's growing internationally respected environmental ethos. The soon-to-be-acclaimed Spretnak read from her landmark work *Lost Goddesses of Early Greece: A Collection of Pre-Hellenic Mythology*.[88]

Lawrence Ferlinghetti
Photograph by
Peter Haase

Enter Lawrence Ferlinghetti

There was never any doubt that Sylvia Beach was the spiritual godmother of the Literary Storefront. That's how it was. In New York, Frances Steloff had demonstrated that women could thrive in the mannish book world of North America, no argument there. If there was a politically or poetically sympathetic individual that the Literary Storefront community wanted to jam with in flagrante though, Lawrence Ferlinghetti from San Francisco was number one with a bullet.

The Writing in Our Time: Seven Benefit Readings for West Coast Literary Presses,[89] a series coordinated by Warren Tallman and his Poetry Center, brought Ferlinghetti to the city on March 16, 1979, along with Margaret Laurence, Brian Fawcett and Robert Kroetsch.[90] These highly anticipated events drew audiences of up to 850 people, with each event featuring four big-name writers, and ran from February until August at the Italian Cultural Centre. The series was subtitled "the best of times, the worst of times": authors were to discuss their best and worst fears as artists and their hopes and fears for writing in our time. The schedule included Robert Creeley, Diane di Prima, Margaret Atwood, Gary Snyder, Anne Waldman, Fred Wah, Marian Engel, bpNichol, Allen Ginsberg, Victor Coleman, Daphne Marlatt and Edward Dorn. Vancouver newspapers had devoted a slew of publicity that protested attacks made in Parliament on poet bill bissett's work, on Talonbooks for having published some of it and on the Canada Council for supporting publication of what political critics were calling obscene material.[91] It was a turbulent issue as Cathy Ford remembers:

The Writing in Our Time benefits were important in banding together writers, readers and publishers in the Vancouver area and B.C. Bill bissett suffered more than most of us knew, I think—he was so capable of mesmerizing an audience, especially those who had never had opportunity to hear him read before. I don't remember whether James Reaney read the same night his wife, Colleen Thibeaudeau did; but his work struck me very hard later on. Colleen took the roof off the Italian Centre. She coherently and politically addressed the importance of bill's work to us all, not just as writers, but as Canadians. How uplifting![92]

Not all were excited with the selection of writers on the bill. On February 16, 1979, Dorothy Livesay, who was living on Galiano Island, wrote an Open Letter to Karl Siegler:

I am glad to hear of the campaign by the Vancouver Poetry Centre to find support for Talonbooks community effort rather than depend on a government body. In the Thirties' days we had to do our own thing—or perish. Often we perished!

What I feel unhappy about in the series . . . is the disproportion given between men and women writers. Out of twenty-seven listed, there are only four women—and only two of them are Canadian . . . so why cannot we hear their voices?... Instead of having half the programs devoted to Americans who have long since outlived their "movement." It's time Vancouver stopped being so old hat. It's dangerous also. Just as the best Canadian playwrights are giving us a vital mirror of ourselves today, so are the best Canadian poets! We do not need a branch plant culture.[93]

The Vancouver Poetry Centre was a non-profit society that had functioned since 1960 with Warren Tallman as chair and Bill Horne as coordinator. In a widely discussed action, it had taken out a full-page advertisement in the *Vancouver Sun*, titling it "Vox Populi for a Poet and His Publisher," signed by 434 names, each paying a maximum of $10. As Mona remembers:

I had previously written and invited Lawrence Ferlinghetti to read. In my correspondence, I had expressed how City Lights was one of the important beacons in inspiring the creation of the Literary Storefront. When Warren Tallman heard that Ferlinghetti had accepted my invitation, he was not amused. Tallman was determined that I should cancel the reading—and he could be very intimidating. I stood my ground and asked Keith Maillard, the B.C. Rep of TWUC to back me in the dispute. He proceeded to act as a mediator between Tallman and myself and gave me much-needed support. Keith spoke with Tallman; he helped a lot.

The Storefront reading was not cancelled, and the following evening, on St Patrick's Day, Ferlinghetti read there in sympathy with its aims and operating style. Every nook and cranny was crammed for his second appearance in two days in Vancouver, and the evening had the decided feel that this elder of the tribe was genuinely bestowing his authentication on the literary centre he had in part inspired by his example in San Francisco. Years later on Salt Spring, Peter Haase remembers:

Allan Twigg, bill bissett

We packed the place. When we closed the doors, I was on the bar at the back, selling drinks and books—I did that for years. When Mona brought Lawrence Ferlinghetti in, he understood that his City Lights Books had been a major influence on the style of things at the Storefront, and he was grinning like the cat that swallowed the canary. We had a lot of those kinds of events.[94]

For those present that night, it was truly memorable; a great presence from the world poetry family had arrived among them. It was not a casual visit. Few writers of Ferlinghetti's generation matched his visceral anti-authoritarian and political commitment, ensuring that his reading appearance was marked by dynamic intensity. Ferlinghetti behaved graciously and read and spoke for an hour.

Poet Nellie McClung, granddaughter of the early twentieth-century Canadian feminist, social activist and politician of the same name, kept a record of the evening that bloomed as a poem. It appeared in the Storefront newsletter:

An Evening Spent With Ferlinghetti
—Nellie McClung

Tallman said
which poet do you
admire most
Li Po, I said &
Dylan Thomas
among the dead but
Ferlinghetti is the
greatest living poet.
Fine, said Tallman,
copy him. So I sat
down and wrote my
art poems. So I was
on the wings of silver air
the nite I went to hear
Ferlinghetti read on St.
Patrick's Day at the
Literary Storefront
Mona Fertig had copied after
Sylvia Beach's Shakespeare &
Company in Paris with pix of
Ezra, James J., Djuna Barnes,
I dove into the Pizza Patio
the bar below at 131 Water Street
an hour ahead of time
Mona with her new string hair
& Peter & Evelyn were sitting having
apricot brandies. I've met him
said Evelyn, he looks like a Russian
count with a trim grey beard, I told
him I hadn't read his poetry but he
said fine that was true of most
audiences, he liked it that way,
then we went upstairs to Room 213
with a stuffed doll of Sylvia Beach

in the window & waited for the
great one to arrive. I sat prominently
in the front row on this most auspicious
occasion of 1979. Promptly at 8:30 he arrived
with a pretty blonde with straight hair
on his arm, in black peasant blouse
costume, he wore a white line sports shirt
brown corduroys & carried a Greenpeace
bag. He thoughtfully varied his program
from the night before on the Talonbooks
Fund Raising series, since we were sitting
like magpies at both readings, there was
Brian Fawcett the Socred millionaire's son
who has just discovered the poor & the Left
& would have us do so along with him
Robert Kroetsch who has been dipping into
seed catalogues Colleen Thibaudeau who
had us singing like moulting canaries
which was a never-to-forget experience
for me & 1,000 other squawking moulting canaries
& Ferlinghetti who was super-cool
relaxed says he likes Canadians.
He stole the show of course & then he
& Paula for that turned out to be her name
sat up till 3 a.m. for the dancing.
Saturday nite at the Storefront it was
predictably packed with youth intelligentsia.
He read from Coney Island of the Mind
with many a discussion about the poems
says he doesn't want to be a poet
with a ten-minute introduction to a
two-minute poem. Also says Jack Spicer
said if you want to write editorials
keep them for the newspapers not poems.
Sound advice said Ferlinghetti. Then after
three quarters of an hour he sat beside the bar.
I had just $2 in my purse but I bought

my fifth Coney Island of the Mind
which I took up to have autographed
on my favourite poem 'The Wounded Wilderness
of Morris Graves.' I asked him if he
ever received my book Baraka which I had
whipped off to him last November.
He said is your name Nellie, my heart
lost a beat, he had it on his shelves,
hadn't read it yet, but would now
    ... then Ferlinghetti went
& sat down on the couch. He told us he
had sent his poem to Morris Graves
but never received a reply, is he dead
someone said, don't know (he lives)
then Ferlinghetti began to get glassy
eyes the kind poets get when they want
to get away, it was 11 p.m. & he had
his arm around the blond companion.
Then Armand offered him a ride & my
heart quickened maybe we were all going
out together what I had spent 2 hours
planning but once on the street Armand
said Sorry Nellie there's just room
for four so they went west down Gastown
the four of them discussing where
they were going to eat, my party,
& I went east into the nite, lonely,
on the way home on the bus I contented
myself by thumbing Coney Island for the
110th time. Sunday I phoned for Wylo she
said they had gone to La Brasserie
& discussed black holes in space in
poetry then went back to Tallman's &
split a bottle of champagne but
somehow it wasn't the same.

        —Vancouver, March 17, 1979

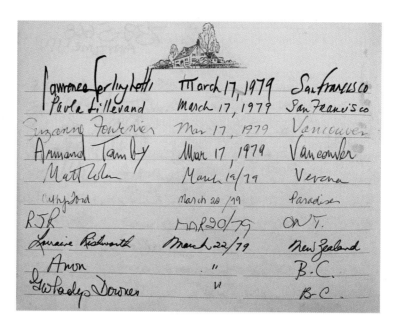

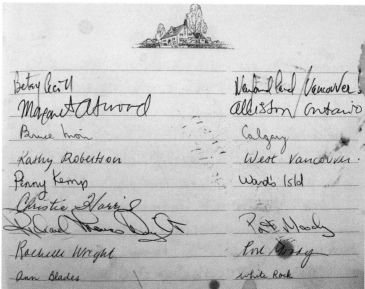

Signatures from
guest book

Margaret Atwood reading

A Night with Margaret Atwood

Batting in the cleanup position came an evening reading with
Margaret Atwood on October 20, 1979, that revealed how formidably
the arc of her career was trending. Atwood had lived in Vancouver
while working as a lecturer at UBC during the early '60s and had strong
affiliations with the city. She maintained ties with a good number of
its writers, notably the lesbian novelist Jane Rule of *Desert of the Heart*
fame and her partner, UBC professor Helen Sonthoff, enthusiastic
teacher and scholar of Canadian literature. Atwood had lived in rented
digs in Point Grey, and during that time, she wrote the first draft of her

Margaret Atwood signing
guest book, Mona Fertig

early novel *The Edible Woman* and some of
the poems in her collection *The Circle Game*.[95]
She had also been published early on in her
career by bill bissett's blewointment press.
Atwood had cultivated an audience for her
fiction and poetry through regular reading
appearances at colleges, and had cemented
a formidable critical reputation in 1972 with
her *Survival: A Thematic Guide to Canadian
Literature*.

Atwood's appearance was much anticipated. In addition to her writerly work, she
had compounded her growing accomplish-
ments with a strong political engagement with feminism, and with
environmental and social justice issues. She stood up and spoke when
it counted. Her feminist ethos and literary concern with identity were
becoming concrete symbols for a generation of younger women
poets and writers, especially in pointing out how it was possible to
transcend traditional colonial and male-focused literary, political and
cultural tropes. With a reading and speaking style that could veer
cannily from coy to prickly, Atwood intended to read from her new
work, *Life Before Man*, that was already being called her most fully
realized novel. "Only 100 tickets in total" were available at $3 and $4.
"Come early if you don't want to sit on the floor, we have a limited
amount of chairs," the Storefront's promo touted.

Vancouver responded with a jam-packed house. Autographed
copies of the book were on sale for $12.95. Claudia Cornwall recalls:

I remember when Margaret Atwood came; she was standing
in front of the podium, and there was quite a gap between her and
the audience. She asked if the audience could all move forward, and
that took plenty of shuffling and rearranging. I remember thinking
it would have been easier for her to move her podium![96]

As the Kingston Trio and later Frank Sinatra had it, 1979 was a very good year. By the end, the Storefront was solvent and doing well. Income from all sources was $16,735.39. Expenditures, including Fertig's minimal salary of $2,763.41, were $16,502.03, resulting in a balance forward to the 1980 budget of $233.36. Ironically, despite this good outcome and shortly prior to Atwood's arrival, news befell the Storefront that it might have to move.

The Move

Fertig wrote in the November 1979 newsletter that Charterhouse Properties, the new owners of Gaslight Square, did not envision the literary centre in its long-term plans for a fashionable courtyard of shops and lawyers' offices. The search was on for a new location. Granville Island or Kitsilano were preferred given the number of members who lived west of Main Street; the Kits district, which during the brief heyday of hippie culture in the mid and late '60s had seen 4th Avenue blossom as Love Street, was still relatively affordable. On November 9, Charterhouse gave Fertig and the Storefront thirty days' notice to leave. "I went to a lawyer after I'd recovered from my hangover and found out that it was an illegal notice."[97] That meant a month's extension, so the move could be stalled until January. But Fertig felt it was better to bite the bullet and clear out, to store things and take until the end of January to find new digs. It would be, she wrote, an opportunity "to sit on some great 1980 ideas."

Calls were put out for volunteers, storage space and a van to help move. After December 15, mail would be directed to General Delivery, Main Post Office on West Georgia Street. The Writers' Union also redirected their mail to the B.C. Rep's home address. In determining needs for the next Storefront space, Fertig stated, "We need 1,000 sq. feet (at least), 1st or 2nd floor, near a good bus route and not more than $275.00 a month." The Storefront was also willing to share space

New Play Centre reading

with another arts group.[98]

One possible new location—which still stands in Gastown—was situated near the corner of Cambie on West Cordova. Putting a brave face on things, Fertig asserted that the Storefront would be ready to open again by February. She added:

Keep the memberships, poems and book reviews coming. The Storefront's first year and eight months have been eventful to say the least. We have survived the past eight months without government funding although we do need more money. We now have about 290 members and 60 newsletter subscribers. Our purpose is to provide a center, a place, a focus for the literary arts.[99]

By the end of 1979, the Storefront could, with a sense of pride and vindication, proclaim that it had presented readings, talks and workshops with a bumper harvest of literary figures, including Anne Szumigalski from Saskatchewan, Mark Madoff from New York, An Evening of Pat Lowther, plus Rikki, Cathy Ford, Maxine Gadd and investigative language poet Leslie Scalapino from Berkeley.

Book sale
Photograph by
Milton Bingham

QUALITY
BOOK
SALE

SUNDAY, NOVEMBER 30
Noon to 6:00 pm
#1 - 314 West Cordova

Proceeds to:
THE LITERARY STOREFRONT
THE WRITERS' UNION OF CANADA
THE LEAGUE OF CANADIAN POETS

BOOK DONATIONS GREATLY APPRECIATED — 688-0711

It had hosted writing work-shops and courses on erotic litera-ture, playwriting, television drama writing, poetry and short fiction. Other offerings had included films, open readings, publication parties, exhibits, feedback sessions, script readings and a book sale.

As ever, there was the stuffed homage to inspiring guru Sylvia Beach in the window. It had been a wild ride—and it had only just begun.

David Watmough
Photograph by
Milton Bingham

5

1980: Renewed Advance
and Timely New Digs

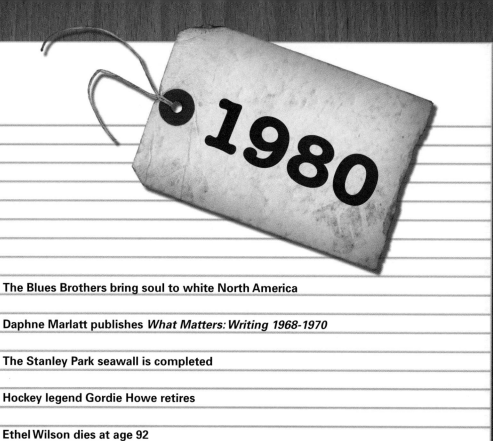

1980

The Blues Brothers bring soul to white North America

Daphne Marlatt publishes *What Matters: Writing 1968-1970*

The Stanley Park seawall is completed

Hockey legend Gordie Howe retires

Ethel Wilson dies at age 92

Terry Fox gains immortality with his cross-Canada Marathon of Hope

Solidarity Trade Union formed in Poland

Tennessee Williams is writer-in-residence at UBC

Ronald Reagan elected U.S. President

John Lennon murdered in New York

bill bissett publishes *soul arrow*

Mount St. Helens blows her stacks

By February 1980, the new location was clear. After many weekends
of walking through the quiet city warehouse streets searching
for storefront and office space, with newly hired executive director of
the TWUC BC Branch Ingrid Klassen, Mona found the second floor of
a brick building at #1-314 West Cordova Street. It was a 2,000-square-
foot space with two offices at the back, a small dark washroom, more
than enough open space for events and a three-year lease. Fertig signed
on February 28 for $264.91 monthly, but the Cordova location had
utilities and operating costs of $181.34 that totalled $446.25. It was
best rental space available, and realistically the Storefront's operations were already running out of space at the first location. It made
sense to relocate. The new space was even large enough to consider
sharing the expenses with other associations. "We want to rent one,
possibly two of the offices to a group or an individual who wants a
space," Fertig wrote in the February newsletter. "Approx. $90 and $60
a month; includes heat and light."

The Writers' Union of Canada had started its B.C. regional office
in the Storefront's first location on a trial basis of three months, October to December 1978. After discussions with Fertig, TWUC decided

2nd Storefront
top floor of 314
W. Cordova
Photograph by
Mark Hand

Moving in day
Photograph by
Milton Bingham

to search for new space with Mona and rented the largest and nicest office at the back of the Cordova Street site. Ingrid Klassen's office had a large window overlooking a part of the alleyway behind the building with plenty of red brick.

In a temporary crisis of identity due to its second-floor site, the operation was no longer a "storefront," and the name vacillated between the Literary Storefront and the Literary Centre. For a time it was both.

Move in began immediately, and the official reopening was Saturday, March 1, 1980, with a gala party and reading co-organized with the B.C. members of TWUC. Headlining the Canada Council-sponsored evening bash were Sylvia Fraser, Graeme Gibson, Keith Maillard, Brian Moore and Susan Musgrave. The large loft space

Re-opening of The Literary Storefront: Keith Maillard, Graham Gibson (back), Sylvia Fraser, Brian Moore, Susan Musgrave, Mona Fertig, Photograph by Richard Wright

was jammed with people. Peter handled the bar. The Storefront was back with a bang.

It was a cosmically fortunate bang. Fertig had truly turned up a four-leaf clover when she found the Cordova Street space. Bill Jeffries, who was part of the artists' collective TBA-TV (Television By Artists) that occupied the space above the Literary Storefront from 1979 to 1989,[100] recalls the generous nature of the proprietor, Mr. Thompson:

The Thompson family owned a lot of real estate—whole city blocks downtown . . . The upshot of all this was that we paid about $1.50 a square foot at a time when the market rate was about $8. Had a place like the Literary Storefront not effectively had a rent-subsidized space, they just wouldn't have been able to make it. Mind you, they had more space than we ever used. They must have had 1,800 square feet at least. I had 600 square feet [for the] Coburg Gallery, 900 square feet in total. It was totally an exciting time in the arts community itself. The art scene itself was in fairly good shape.[101]

Jan Westendorp, another member of the artists' cooperative upstairs, recalls the upbeat energy that the Storefront brought to its new address:

I was delighted when the Literary Storefront moved into 314 West Cordova Street. No longer was TBA-TV the building's only tenant, we had the company of another arts group.[102]

Business continued as before. Mona continued to work long hours organizing and co-ordinating, fundraising, hosting and promoting and with Peter helping out at events per usual, singing or handling book sales and door admission. Regular volunteer meetings discussed the need for rotating reading hosts, ideas regarding the sale of books by members and B.C. writers, new hours, "a creative working collective" and so on. Volunteers were called; six to ten people were needed monthly to assist with a two-hour newsletter mail-out session.

Some people criticized the Storefront's location because of the empty stores downstairs and the general lack of street lighting, but Fertig preferred it to the old location in Gaslight Square, which she felt was "too commercial." In an interview for *Vancouver Magazine* with Dona Sturmanis, she observed:

There was no communication with the shopkeepers; they didn't understand what we were doing. It may seem spooky, but the new location is actually very safe and more in character with what we really are—creative, not commercial. And everything is within reach: the bookstores, the copy machine, the liquor store.[103]

Peter Haase recalls the transformation:

We moved further up, above the Triangle Restaurant on the corner of Cambie and Cordova Street. We shared our space with The Writers' Union of Canada, with Erik Nordholm who had his little printing shop and others. It was a massive space this time. Cabbages and Kinx clothing shop was right beneath us. We had a great neighbourhood. Across the street, there was the El Cid Hotel pub, and we used to go over for lunch breaks and things, you know, have fish and chips and a pint. In the evenings, of course, there'd be a few iffy characters. They'd come upstairs and barge into the readings. I'd have to politely ask 'em leave. So I was the short-ass bouncer and the bartender. We'd have wine and beer, and like I say, if someone lit up a joint, it got passed around. No hassle for anybody. We all smoked in those days anyway—smoked like chimneys. We'd close the doors, and people would have a wonderful, happy time . . . People would *listen*. We'd have all sorts of improv nights. On one Saturday night after the usual reading/performance event was over, as I did on most weekends, I pulled out my guitar and started

LITERARY STOREFRONT BIRTHDAY BOOK, 1980

The Birthday Book
1980

PETER BEAUDIN ☐ KAREN BODLAK ☐ JAN CONN ☐ FRANCES DUNCAN ☐ MONA FERTIG ☐ CATHY FORD ☐ DAVID FRITH ☐ MAXINE GADD ☐ ELIZABETH GOURLAY ☐ ELDON GRIER ☐ PHIL HALL ☐ S.L. HARMAN ☐ HOSEA HIRATA ☐ SHERALI HUSSEIN ☐ LOUISE HYNDES ☐ CAROLE ITTER ☐ BETH JANKOLA ☐ R.A. KAWALILAK ☐ SCOTT LAWRANCE ☐ KEN LESTER ☐ JO MCBRIDE ☐ SHEILA MCCARTHY ☐ KEITH MAILLARD ☐ CAT MAJORS ☐ JEAN MALLINSON ☐ ANNE MILES ☐ DAVID W. MILLER ☐ COLIN MORTON ☐ FRANCESCA NEWTON-MOSS ☐ MAUREEN NICHOLSON ☐ PASQUALE PASCUCCI ☐ MARGUERITE PINNEY ☐ DAVID PRITCHETT ☐ RENEE RODIN ☐ STANLEY WM. ROGAL ☐ SANDRA G. SHREVE ☐ EMILY SION ☐ K.O. KANE ☐ PHILIP THATCHER ☐ ROSE-MARIE TREMBLAY ☐ ROBERT TYHURST ☐ ANN YORK ☐ CAROLYN ZONAILO ☐ PETER BEAUDIN ☐ KAREN BODLAK ☐ JAN CONN ☐ FRANCES DUNCAN ☐ MONA FERTIG ☐ CATHY FORD ☐ DAVID FRITH ☐ MAXINE GADD ☐ ELIZABETH GOURLAY ☐ ELDON GRIER ☐ PHIL HALL ☐ S.L. HARMAN ☐ HOSEA HIRATA ☐ SHERALI HUSSEIN ☐ LOUISE HYNDES ☐ CAROLE ITTER ☐ BETH JANKOLA ☐ R.A. KAWALILAK ☐ SCOTT LAWRANCE ☐ KEN LESTER ☐ JO MCBRIDE ☐ SHEILA MCCARTHY ☐ KEITH MAILLARD ☐ CAT MAJORS ☐ JEAN MALLINSON ☐ ANNE MILES ☐ DAVID W. MILLER ☐ COLIN MORTON ☐ FRANCESCA NEWTON-MOSS ☐ MAUREEN NICHOLSON ☐ PASQUALE PASCUCCI ☐ MARGUERITE PINNEY ☐ DAVID PRITCHETT ☐ RENEE RODIN ☐ STANLEY WM. ROGAL ☐ SANDRA G. SHREVE ☐ EMILY SION ☐ K.O. KANE ☐ PHILIP THATCHER ☐ ROSE-MARIE TREMBLAY ☐ ROBERT TYHURST ☐ ANN YORK ☐ CAROLYN ZONAILO ☐ PETER BEAUDIN ☐ KAREN BODLAK

Second Birthday Book

up with something that everyone was familiar with. People usually got up dancing at the drop of a hat, and at that perfect moment, Roy Kiyooka started hammering away on one of the bongo drums that we kept in the music box. Anyone could start jamming with the groove of the moment. Peter Trower was also sitting back, like the rest of us, half-inebriated . . . Jamming, singing, dancing—the place was always rocking on a Saturday night.[104]

It was a busy time all around.

The spring workshop schedule was published, with sessions limited to fifteen participants each. The topics would be Journalism with Andreas Schroeder; Science Fiction with Susan Wood, the well-known speculative or science fiction writer and professor (who died later that year; one of her students was William Gibson); Jane Rule leading Autobiographical Writing; Book Reviewing with Eleanor Wachtel; and Short Fiction with Audrey Thomas. And there was a Blackfish Press reading with Alan Safarik, Joe Rosenblatt, Albert Moritz and Jim Green.

In May, publication of the second annual *Birthday Book* was underway, again comprising poetry (eighty lines maximum), short prose (600 words) and literary-related visual images in black and white, including photographs. Successful entrants received two copies of the limited edition of 400. George Payerle oversaw direction of the typography of this second edition set in Itek Bembo, and Mona Fertig and Phil Hall were the editors. The volume had the look of a small press chapbook of the 1960s.[ix]

---

ix   In the mix of veteran and newer contributors were Peter Beaudin, Karen Bodlak, Jan Conn, Sandy Frances Duncan , David Frith, Elizabeth Gourlay, Eldon Grier, Phil Hall, Hosea Hirata, Sherali Hussien, R.A. Kawalilak, Carole Itter, Beth Jankola, Ken Lester, Shelia McCarthy, Keith Maillard, Colin Morton, Francesca Newton-Moss, Pasquale Pascucci, Marguerite Pinney, Renee Rodin, Stan Rogal, Robert Tyhurst, Ann York, Sandra Shreve, Emily Sion and Rose-Marie Tremblay.

The following untitled poem is by Marguerite Pinney, one of the forty-three contributors.

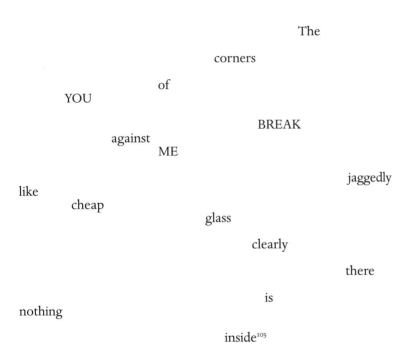

But the big news was a very special event, a great big bash: the B.C. Writers' Review was set for May 7 at the city's premier venue, the Queen Elizabeth Playhouse. Teaming up with The Writers' Union, Fertig, Maillard and Klassen capitalized on May's National Book Festival to line up fifteen writers for a two-hour literary show interspersed with music by Kathy Kidd and Jim McGillveray, musical direction by the young guitarist Stephen Nikleva (a future member of Petunia and the Vipers) and special guest Ferron, who was to become one of the West Coast's most popular folksinger/songwriters. A book

B.C. Writers' Review
poster

table and autograph party were set up for afterwards. Tickets were $3 and $4. Maggi Shore designed the yellow poster. Headliners for the gala fundraiser were Earle Birney,[106] bill bissett, Dorothy Livesay, David Watmough, Susan Musgrave, Maxine Gadd, Robin Skelton, Christie Harris, Richard Wright, Carol Shields, Robert Harlow and Sandy Frances Duncan. Phyllis Webb cancelled. Octopus Books and Peregrine Books on 4th Avenue in Kitsilano joined other outlets in selling tickets for the big one.

The show took weeks to organize. Keith Maillard, who had previous experience with club dates as a folksinger, took the reins and with Mona and Ingrid chose the writers. They selected excerpts of each writer's work and scripted the show so that the text by each writer would play off the next author. Ferron would sing a related song between every few writers, and there was also synthesized music during the readings. There were a few bumps with stubborn authors Earle Birney and Dorothy Livesay. Both refused to be on stage together, until the curtain call, and wouldn't read what was scripted, but chose something else. Robin Skelton and Susan Musgrave changed the requested poems to poems of their own choice. But everything still worked out, even the unscripted drama when Bob Harlow forgot his place and the synthesized music kept thumping out a heartbeat; no one really noticed it, they thought his pause was part of the show.[107]

It was an unprecedented West Coast literary production. The evening began with a tribute to three of the finest novels written in or about B.C.—excerpt readings from Malcolm Lowry's *Under The Volcano*, Sheila Watson's *The Double Hook* and Howard O'Hagen's *Tay John*. A crowd of almost 450 people attended, and the readings and music went off without a noticeable hitch, prompting a review in *Maclean's* that called it "a spirited and surprisingly professional evening of readings and songs by twelve B.C. authors." CBC *Arts National* covered the program, and Milton Bingham, the Literary Storefront photographer, took what became the famous photograph of all the writers on stage taking their bows and kudos with Mona, Ingrid and Keith joining the conga line.

It was an all-star event. After the show, posters were signed by the writers, everyone mingled, drinking beer and wine, and a great time was had by all in the theatre's tony foyer.

When all the reckoning was done—even with ticket sales, National Book Festival funding of $2,000 and Canada Council readings support of $975—due to basic production costs and venue overhead, the review just broke even.[108] Plus ça change . . .

Clusterings

The Writers' Union of Canada: BC/Yukon Branch

Jane Rule wrote the first draft of the job description for the executive director of the TWUC BC Branch, and Ingrid Klassen's name appeared in the Storefront newsletter in November 1979 as the first paid E.D. "TWUC was a wonderful, dynamic group of people at the time," Klassen remembers, "everyone was passionate about writing." She had already made her way to the Storefront through her work as

"Musical Counterpoint for National Book Festival Week will be the B.C. Writers' Review: in rehearsal here, from left, are musicians Kathy Kidd and Jim McGillveray, authors Robert Harlow and Christie Harris, musical director Stephen Nikleva, and folksinger/songwriter Ferron," photographer unknown, *Vancouver Sun* article by Leslie Peterson

a literary program host for *The Book Show* with CFRO Co-op Radio.[109] She observes:

> The publisher's reps contacted me. We arranged interviews with anyone who had a new book—Margaret Atwood, Carol Shields, Alice Munro, whoever . . . That was the format—always an interview, and music or tapes/recordings from events around town or elsewhere— Capilano College, UBC, a conference in San Francisco . . . I made a room in my apartment into a studio where I could edit reel-to-reel tapes.[110]

B.C. Writers' Review, Q.E. Playhouse:
Ingrid Klassen, Keith Maillaird, Sandy Frances Duncan, Robert Harlow, Robin Skelton, David Watmough,
Maxine Gadd, Dorothy Livesay, Ferron, bill bissett, Earle Birney, Susan Musgrave, Christie Harris, Richard
Wright, Carol Shields, Mona Fertig

Robin Skelton

Ferron

Earle Birney

Photographs by Milton Bingham

Mona Fertig,
Ingrid Klassen

Klassen confirms that inquiries at the TWUC office seemed to come in waves, then would quiet a little. In response, the BC Branch prepared a booklet that answered general questions concerning publishing, copyright, agents, multiple submissions, royalties and advances. At a price of 50 cents, it was a fabulous deal.

The Storefront was conducive for literary encounters of all kinds. Fertig remembers novelist Blanche Howard telling her how she met Carol Shields at the Literary Storefront through TWUC. They were to become great friends:

Carol and I became active participants in the still fledgling BC chapter of The Writers' Union of Canada. The meetings were informal and we were frequently entertained by the music of Keith Maillard and his guitar or by somewhat unrestrained partying, often at the beautiful home of Jan Drabek and his tolerant wife Joan.[III]

For TWUC members, linking with the Storefront made good sense. They had a Vancouver space to call home, rather than having to book a red-eye flight to Toronto for the pilgrimage to Hogtown's premises for writers at 24 Ryerson Avenue, off Queen Street. Teaming up with the Storefront made organizing readings and book promotional events that much easier. During the fall book season in October, TWUC decided to go flat out and host a press party to unveil new publications by B.C. members of the Union. The end-of-business-day 5-to-8 PM affair was an informal meet-and-greet with authors and publisher representatives, and marked a new level of seriousness. Where previously authors would meet with a local newspaper columnist at a business account bar or restaurant with a publisher's aide in tow, the new TWUC space was a chance for a larger communal schmooze. The Gastown location helped, of course; there was no shortage of amiable pubs nearby to continue the evening's mill and swill.

For Klassen, the TWUC enterprise lasted two years until she was receiving more hours at Octopus Books, her main source of income.

Dallas Peterson Associates

A further salutary development occurred in the spring of 1980 when a new literary business service struck up alliance with the Storefront. Dallas Peterson Associates, which included Orca Sound Publishing[112] and the Write People—"an association of professional editors, writers, teachers, researchers, and consultants experienced in literary services" headed by UBC graduate Dona Sturmanis—sublet the second back office space at the new Storefront premises. The new operation also offered ghostwriting, graphic design and layout. With Monday to Friday 12-to-5 PM hours that the nighthawk Sturmanis would soon expand to 8 PM, the service brought the Storefront space further activity. A freelance writer and poet herself, Sturmanis was hopeful that the Periodical Writers Association of Canada (PWAC) would take a share of the service's office and help with the rent, and this proved the case. "We are a business, not a society, so we charge for our work," the new outfit's brochure copy ran. "Our rates are reasonable and competitive."

Like Ingrid Klassen, Sturmanis became an identifiable Storefront community fixture. By providing a literary services division that helped place books in public library collections, her brainchild truly helped serve as "a complete service for writers"—and worked in tandem with the Storefront's mission. In addition to regular Storefront activities and Writers' Union activities, anyone seeking help or information about writing and publishing from Dallas Peterson Associates could expect to be informed about "tutorials and classes in writing technique; analysis of style and form; editing, revision, organization; preparation of manuscripts; ghostwriting and research; procedural instructions for submission; marketing recommendations; [and] translation." Sturmanis's printer partner Erik Nordholm also joined her there. Later they brought their baby in while they worked. They had an AB Dick 330 printing press and did offset jobs, and writing and design for the Storefront and others. The third Literary Storefront *Birthday Book* was printed and published by Orca Sound Publications in 1982.

The new service also offered expertise for both novice and experienced writers regarding writing articles for magazines and newspapers, non-fiction books, how-to and trade publications, reports and manuals, short stories for literary and consumer magazines, poetry and literary and commercial novels. The Storefront space was now the closest thing that Vancouver and the West Coast had seen to a fully functioning, one-stop literary centre for educational and professional development.

The League of Canadian Poets

The League of Canadian Poets (LCP) opened a part-time office in September 1980. Phil Hall was the first poet who kept League hours, Tuesdays 10-5 PM; later it was Lorraine Vernon, who was the B.C. Rep and office person. Like The Writers' Union in the first Store-

Mona Fertig,
Dona Sturmanis

front location, they sat at Mona's desk and looked after questions
about publishing and marketing poetry and answered the phone
one afternoon a week. They also offered B.C. members a chance to
participate in Poets in the Schools readings. The Writers' Union had
by now graduated to their own comfortable office in the back. The
TWUC and LCP offices were the first regional representation for these
national organizations. Cathy Ford, former president of LCP, recalls:

Unfortunately for the League of Canadian Poets, it was entering
into dark financial days, and the out-reach effort through the Literary
Storefront was unable to survive when the volunteers faded, and likely,
the Toronto office eliminated even the barest funding support. Like
TWUC, the LCP had its largest group of members outside Toronto,
and/or Ontario, in B.C. The most dedicated League volunteer, Lorraine Vernon, kept things going until she moved full-time to Galiano
Island.[113]

The Periodical Writers Association of Canada

The Periodical Writers Association of Canada, today known as the Professional Writers Association of Canada (PWAC), had joined the potpourri and began holding its monthly meetings at the new Storefront location, bringing magazine and periodical writers into the fold.

Active members included arts and food specialist James Barber, magazine feature writer Daniel Wood, wickedly ascerbic lifestyle specialist Eve Rockett, investigative reporter Mark Budgen, multi-media specialist Ann Bishop and media critic Donald Gutstein. Like TWUC members, PWAC writers were geared to securing better working conditions and payment from publishers, and they wilfully broke the code of silence that publishers had long urged in their individual contract dealings with writers; PWAC members freely shared the going rates for freelance articles and projects with publications across the country. At last it became easier for freelance writers to get a better deal and perhaps, astoundingly, to survive or even thrive as working writers. PWAC also began the path-breaking work of inviting magazine, journal, newspaper and electronic media editors to meetings with writers. In the age of the typewriter, it went on to organize some of the earliest seminars for writers and business people in Vancouver in the still early development use of "word processors," including a special evening that left attendees stunned on "The Source"—an astounding electronic network of information linked to major U.S. and British libraries, an early prototype of what would become recognizable as the Internet.

The Federation of British Columbia Writers

The Literary Storefront's energy also sparked the birth of the Federation of British Columbia Writers. Novelist and short story writer Sandy Frances Duncan recalls:

In the spring of 1980 I took over from Keith Maillard as B.C.

Representative of The Writers' Union of Canada, inheriting the newly established B.C. office; a desk in the back room of the Literary Storefront. Ingrid Klassen . . .; she worked one day a week . . . Some of us thought we needed a regional group to represent all writers—playwrights, poets, journalists and so on—in addition to trade book writing, [as] the members of TWUC. In the fall I phoned the representatives of all the writers' groups I could find and set up an exploratory meeting on the Storefront's overstuffed chairs and sofas. Enough people came so we had to unseat Sylvia Beach. She accepted the corner of the floor with her usual patience and dignity and after the meeting I put her back in her chair. Fourteen months and many meetings later, the Federation of British Columbia Writers started work.[114]

Given the heightened degree of reading, learning and networking opportunity that was in the air, an item in the September 1980 newsletter tellingly brought word that "the Federation of British Columbia Writers," an organization hoping to represent all professional writers in all genres, would shortly be soliciting qualified members from throughout the province. The Federation was to be constituted like existing provincial writers' guilds in Alberta, Saskatchewan and Nova Scotia. For writers who had not found their way into national literary organizations, the Fed would be a brand new option for keeping up with developments in the writing and publishing world. It would lead, at time of writing, to a thirty-year opportunity for regional writers. Contacts at this early stage were Sandy Frances Duncan and David Conn, both Literary Storefront members.

The writers who attended inception meetings were Sandy Frances Duncan, James Barber, Carolyn Zonailo, Jan Drabek, Keith Maillard, Frank Gerber, Betty Millway, Michael Mercer, Ross Westergaard, K.O. Kanne, Daniel Wood, Mona Fertig, Trevor Carolan and others. Calgary novelist Aritha van Herk, who was spending a year in Vancouver, also attended meetings frequently and contributed valuable

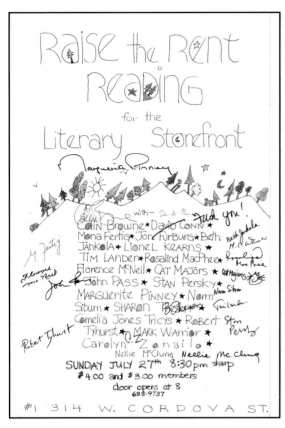

Raise the Rent
poster

information concerning how the Writers Guild of Alberta operated on behalf of writers there. The B.C. members of the Canadian Authors' Association donated seed money to get the Fed off the ground and also use of their non-profit/incorporation number that had lain dormant for a few years.[115]

Among the Fed's goals were to seek funding, to be a non-profit society of professional and aspiring writers and to act as an umbrella organization for writers of fiction, poetry, drama, journalism, non-fiction, magazines and radio/film/television; to achieve common goals on such concerns as copyright laws, payment for public use, photocopying legislation, support for readings and school programs, establishment of a provincial writers' centre and archives and provincial writers' awards, as well as a rural writers' retreat.[116]

In June the Canada Council sponsored a night with Al Neil and Carole Itter, who read short articles and selections from her journals and other pieces. In an evening calculated to "wed right and left brain," the idiosyncratic Neil shared work he had not read previously in public. It was an event that required Itter's skill to keep it all together.

On July 27, a Raise the Rent Reading was held at 8:30 PM, $4 and $3 for members. Mona drew and hand-coloured a poster, with twenty poets featured, including Stan Persky, Nellie McClung, Jon Furberg, John Pass, Marguerite Pinney, Norm Sibum, Tim Lander, Colin Browne and Lionel Kearns.

In the first two years, over 14,000 people had visited the Literary Storefront, attending events such as readings, book sales, workshops, special performances and book launches. By October 1980, the statement showed income of $12,057.79. This included revenue from events and workshops, a book sale, membership dues ($1,930), donations ($439), office rent and phone from TWUC, newsletter subscriptions and several modest-sized project grants from the Vancouver Arts Council ($750), the Leon and Thea Koerner Foundation and the City of Vancouver. Another $3,000 in grants from the Leon and Thea Koerner Foundation and City of Vancouver were on TWUC books, the Storefront's close ally.

The Canada Council came through once again when Roy McSkimming announced its $3,000 contribution toward production of the Storefront's new promotional brochure, an idea that he affirmed was well-received in Ottawa. The 12-page brochure, An Introduction to the Literary Storefront, was mailed first to members, affiliates, funders and media. Designed and written by Cathy Ford, who was now editor and typesetter at Caitlin Press,[117] it named all the Storefront services, its accomplishments to date and its goals. The salmon-coloured cover listed over 200 names of writers who had read. It was an excellent promotional tool.

Glaringly absent in the society's balance sheets was any item of provincial government arts support. Fertig had been informed in 1979 that BC Cultural Grant funding required a minimum of two years of active operations as a non-profit society. As C.M. Thomas, Administrator, Grant Funds, wrote on January 5, 1979, "Customary to receiving local arts council funding a group must establish a history of community financial support prior to receiving direct assistance from the BC Cultural Fund."

In October 1980, The Writers' Union of Canada BC/Yukon Branch, the League of Canadian Poets and the Literary Storefront put in a group application to the BC Cultural Fund for $25,000 to run the Literary Storefront as a Literary Centre. A broad swath of provincial, regional and community literary organizations, as well as individuals, rallied in support of the cause. All were becoming linked through the Storefront's work and understood the vital role it was fulfilling. There would be co-operative programs with TWUC, the LCP, PWAC, the Playwrights Guild of Canada (PGC), the Canadian Book Information Centre and various other writers groups, as well as information-sharing and services with most publishers. Others expected to be involved included the Association of Book Publishers of BC (ABPBC), the Canadian Authors' Association (CAA), the Burnaby Writers' Society, the Richmond Writers Group, the Association of English Teachers of BC and the Canadian Periodical Publishers Association (CPPA). It was an ambitious and unique application.[x] The board of directors of the Literary Centre would be Sandy Frances Duncan (B.C. Rep, TWUC), Robin Skelton (B.C. Rep, LCP), Paulette Kerr (Regional Director, CIBC), Scott McIntyre (publisher, ABPBC) and Margaret Hollingsworth (B.C. Rep, PGC). Administrative staff would be Mona Fertig, founder and managing director of the Literary Storefront, and Ingrid Klassen, executive director of the BC Branch of The Writers' Union of Canada.

An appeal was made to supporters for personal letters to be sent by October 15 to Tom Fielding at the Cultural Services Branch of the Ministry of Provincial Secretary and Government Services. Fielding vetted applications from arts organizations, but under successive Social Credit regimes, the funding climate had been one of austerity. Receiving financial support was not impossible, but it was a serious challenge. Fertig and her allies were depending on a BC Cultural grant

---

x   Support letters also came from Paulette Kerr, regional director of the Canadian Book Information Centre; Linda Turnbull, director of the ABPBC; Leonard Angel, B.C. Rep of the Guild of Canadian Playwrights; Eleanor Wachtel, vice-president of the Canadian Periodical Publishers Association (CPPA); Lorna Farrell-Ward, now curator at the Vancouver Art Gallery; the Vancouver Public Library and many more. Sandy Frances Duncan (TWUC BC Rep) and Mona prepared the application.

to help with rent and operating expenses. Fertig was facing the reality of a situation in which she could not reasonably continue to work as the Storefront's chief executive everything without some form of remuneration. "If this grant does not come through the future of the Storefront is in jeopardy," she wrote in the newsletter. A decision was expected in January.

Meeting Tennessee Williams

Tennessee Williams was writer-in-residence at UBC in 1980, and his play, *The Red Devil Battery Sign*, was on at the Vancouver Playhouse. One day, a Storefront member visited Mona at work and said she should invite Williams to meet some local writers. Mona thought it was a great idea, and the member made the contact. Williams agreed to come in October, and Mona invited about fifteen people to a private soirée at the Storefront, including Alan Twigg, Dorothy Livesay and Maxine Gadd. It was a cold, wet, dark evening. Wine, beer and cheese were readied, and everyone waited. It wasn't long before Williams' assistant called to explain that unfortunately the visit had to be cancelled. Williams, he said, was too exhausted to leave his hotel room. But Tennessee suggested that three writers could come and visit. Mona gathered Dorothy Livesay and Maxine Gadd, and they were driven to the Best Western Plus Sands Hotel on Denman Street, for the visit. Mona remembers:

We were welcomed in to a plain hotel suite by a young man and invited to sit in the living room.[118] Tennessee came out of the bedroom to greet us. He was a short man who seemed considerate and interested in talking to some poets. The young man disappeared into the bedroom. Dorothy began talking to Tennessee about writing, which led to Williams asking us to recite some erotic poetry. Dorothy recited from memory "The Unquiet Bed", I recited my poem "Eros" and Maxine recited a poem as well. We stayed for an hour, then he

Tennessee Williams, 1980,
UBC Archives,
Photograph by Banham
[UBC44.1/25-2]

signed a copy of his novel that I had, *Moise and the Noise of Reason*. Dorothy was excited about meeting him, we all were, and she grinned like a Cheshire cat. Afterwards we happily walked down the dim hotel hallway and downstairs to the bar for a drink before we headed out into the dark rain. It was a night I never forgot.[119]

Three workshops in November brought back *Books in Canada* critic Eleanor Wachtel on Book Reviewing—"I may not know what's good but I know what I like," or How Not to Write a Book Review; Richard Wright offered a comprehensive professional approach to The Mechanics of Publishing; and well-regarded Vancouver playwright Margaret Hollingsworth led Starting a Play.

Book sales were a legitimate fundraiser idea. The affection the Gastown literary centre enjoyed from its supporters meant that donations were sure to comprise quality paperbacks, hardbound books and collector's items such as limited editions, autographed books and so forth. A joint sale of this kind by the Storefront, Writers' Union and League of Poets generated a surprising $1,204.91.

Dorothy Livesay

The September 21 extravaganza, Fall Equinox Festival: New Work and New Voices, ran from noon to midnight. Celebrating the end of summer and the beginning of autumn, the day-long whoop-up was fêted as an incredible day of poetry, prose, song and voice with thirty-nine writers. It featured café-style refreshments and music, with open-mic readings from 11 PM to midnight. Tickets were $5 and $6. Posters for the show were designed by Chris Glynn, who also read, along with what felt like a cast of thousands.[xi] The late-year fundraising surge was capped with news in November that the Leon and Thea Koerner Foundation was giving $1,000 for a Storefront literary weekend and open house in the new year.

xi   Readers were Jennifer Alley, Marilyn Boyle, Anne Cameron, Jan Conn, Judith Copithorne, Claudia Cornwall, Brian Fawcett, Mona Fertig, Cathy Ford, David Frith, Jon Furberg, Gerry Gilbert, Lakshmi Gill, Chris Glynn, Rosemary Hollingshead, K.O. Kanne, R.A. Kawalilak, Roy Kiyooka, Tim Lander, Scott Lawrance, Dorothy Livesay, Cat Majors, Colin Morton, Erin Moure, Jane Munro, Helen Potrebenko, Stephen Scobie, Bill Schermbrucker, Bob Sherrin, Maggie Shore, Dona Sturmanis, Audrey Thomas, Robert Tyhurst, David U.U., Ed Varney, Phyllis Webb, ElJean Wilson, Carolyn Zonailo, Zonko.

As the year drew to a close, The Writers' Union and Canada Council tag-teamed in presenting Harold Horwood and Bill Percy from Nova Scotia. Horwood was the chair of TWUC and a bona fide member of the CanLit lodge. Less serious in tone, the next night on December 7 was a house-rocking show by blues-belter Susie Whiten, a member of the Barrelhouse Blues band, and poet/jazzoid Peter Trower, in town from his Sunshine Coast home at Gibsons.

Adding to this was an all-star lineup that gathered for a Benefit Reading for the 4th Annual San Francisco Women's Poetry Festival. Following the benefit gala, K.O. Kanne, Rosemary Hollingshead, Ferron, Cathy Ford and Fertig headed south (for the second time)[120] and performed at the festival in San Francisco.[xii] According to Fertig, the women's writing and energy they encountered there "blew our minds." Cathy Ford recalls:

We heard in person many of the finest American women poets we had been reading for years . . . [organizer Noni Howard] had a strong sense of political action in terms of women's work, feminism... I loved the many offshoots of publishing I saw—handmade chapbooks, artbooks, visual art treatments of poetry, overtly feminist works, including those by Judy Chicago and Anne Waldman. The Canadian women poets were serious in performing and in their political attentiveness to the situation. We stood out in the grey rain, in the giant auditorium style space, as if we were all short of time to accomplish what we felt was crucially important, what mattered.[121]

As 1980 concluded, the Storefront's catalogue of readers included Sid Stephen, Sue Ann Alderson, Jan Drabek, Christie Harris, Keith Maillard, Ted Collins, film reviewer Mark Harris, Karl Sandor, Doug Beardsley, Mike Doyle and Theresa Kishkan.

---

xii   Readers were Rosemary Hollinghead, Surjeet Kalsey, Louise Hyndes, Jill Rogers, Jan Conn, Jean Mallinson, Kirsten Emmott, Rosalind MacPhee, Jane Munro, K.O. Kanne, Beth Jankola, Cathy Ford, Maxine Gadd, Lorraine Vernon; poster by Beth Jankola.

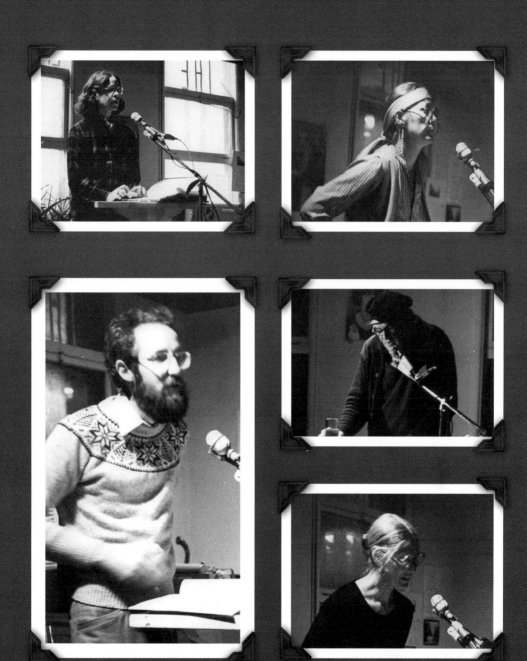

Clockwise from top left:
Judith Copithorne, Anne Cameron. Peter Trower,
Rosemary Hollingshead, Stephen Scobie

Anne Marriott and Carole Itter's *Alphabet*
Photograph by Milton Bingham

6

1981: Remaining Steadfast

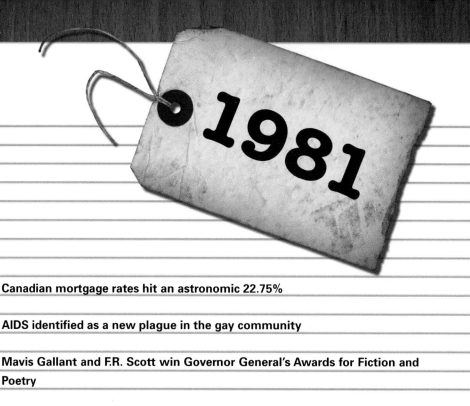

1981

Canadian mortgage rates hit an astronomic 22.75%

AIDS identified as a new plague in the gay community

Mavis Gallant and F.R. Scott win Governor General's Awards for Fiction and Poetry

The Vancouver Aboriginal Friendship Centre opens

Bob Marley dies at 36

Anne Marriott publishes *The Circular Coast*

Bobby Sands dies on prison hunger strike in Northern Ireland

Martial law in Poland

Brixton race riots in London

Vancouver Peace March draws 10,000 people

Joy Kogawa's *Obasan* is published

Quebec's French language sign law comes into effect

The January newsletter explained with regret that the application for provincial funding had not met the response the Storefront had hoped for from the BC Cultural Fund. The Storefront's group application with TWUC and LCP to fund a Literary Centre would receive only $3,000. The sum went towards a phone/answering service, stationary/office expenses, writers-in-schools program, library/tapes/ archives, rent/hydro and program coordinator, for all three groups. It was a bare-bones budget. It did not include funding for anything like an administrative salary. "After all our work and our qualifications, this comes as a big disappointment," Fertig wrote to Tom Fielding on December 19, after receiving notice of the grant. "We are pleased that the Literary Centre has been awarded some money . . . but are surprised at the amount. Did we do something wrong in the submission of our application?" Fielding replied in January, and Mona answered, "It is good to keep the lines of communication open and at times like this we do need feedback. Enclosed is a revised budget and cash flow. At present the Literary groups of B.C. are meeting to decide whether we should federate or not. It may take time to speak with one voice." Colleagues in the arts community suggested that she apply again to the City of Vancouver for a small grant and to the National Book Festival for a fairly high-percentage ask, but the energy required to keep writing and submitting grants, as anyone in arts administration becomes acutely aware, is depleting. "Who wants to write grants all their life! It's absolutely exhausting. Here's to a much better year, we hope," Fertig lamented in the newsletter, using the moment to call yet again for volunteers: "For those of you that want to get involved, to take on a little responsibility, then come down and Volunteer. Set up your own schedule!" Fertig added that she would be available for only two days a week henceforth.[122]

The Storefront's first annual general meeting on January 25 went very well. The volunteers came, and three committees were formed, with five members elected to the society's board. Robert Tyhurst was named liaison for the newsletter committee, Gordon Cornwall for the fundraising committee and Cathy Morton for the readings committee. There was more assistance in sharing the workload now. This would be timely, since Fertig reported that she would be joining poet Cathy Ford in March for a one-month cross-country reading tour. Marilyn Boyle had agreed to keep the Storefront open on Wednesdays from 12 to 4. The Writers' Union and League of Poets would each maintain their regular hours of two afternoons a week. The committee would handle production of the newsletters and readings, while Ingrid Klassen would be handling general mail and memberships. In a small win, it was noted that the Storefront would receive book kits from Ottawa for distribution during the National Book Festival. The 6,000 promotional brochures for the festival produced with Canada Council sponsorship were now also distributed nationally. The date in Vancouver for the annual spring book extravaganza was set for May 14. There was plenty of literary action planned before then. In February, poets Robert Bringhurst and Crispin Elsted appeared. Bringhurst, who had studied at UBC, was gaining attention for his translations, and the interest he shared with Elsted in the revival of the classic ode and elegy. His most recent publication was *Bergschrund*. Elsted hailed from the historic small town of Mission in the Fraser Valley, where he and his wife, Jan, were proprietors of Barbarian Press. Established privately in 1977, it published fine press and limited editions of poetry and translations. Elsted was then working on a long set of his own poems entitled *Crystallography*.

A fortnight later, Andreas Schroeder from Abbotsford, also in the Fraser Valley, was lined up to read from the book that Peter Gzowski of the CBC was making sure the entire country was hearing about. *Shaking It Rough* was Schroeder's nationally acclaimed account of his experience within the federal prison system, after serving his time in B.C. on a charge under the nation's draconian laws on marijuana. Also a poet, he was currently serving as writer-in-residence at the Regina Public Library. Years later he could maintain: "The Literary Storefront was the liveliest, most versatile and best organized literary hangout in Vancouver's cultural scene in the 1970s."[123]

Roy Kiyooka, playing instrument and unknown singing, Bill Schermbrucker in background
Photograph by Peter Haase

As ever, the third-Sunday-of-the-month open readings and informal feedback sessions hosted by Paul Herarty continued to attract a faithful group of fifteen or more writers. In 1981 the Storefront's legacy as a place to take your work downtown or out to the West Coast was firmly cemented. In March Victoria's Marilyn Bowering joined Joe Rosenblatt and Toronto's David Donnell reading from their work. With its ongoing willingness to jam on arts expression in an interdisciplinary way, the centre hosted a performance art production by Fiona McKye and Trudi Forrest, old friends of Mona's from Vancouver School of Art days. This proved an amazing creative event with Fiona (the daughter of Marguerite Pinney who ran special events at the Vancouver Art Gallery) performing a strip of many layers of clothes and styles while Trudi danced and commented with humour and panache in a political statement about women, sexism and personas. Fiona had gained a following for her riveting costume performances to soundtracks of her own design. "I deal with extended identities, sexual ambiguity," she said.[124]

Tim Lander, a West Coast people's poet, whose long global rambles and calm, wise view of things had been tempered by military service in the Malayan jungles, summed up the Storefront's democratic attitude well:

Ingrid Klassen, Dwain Ruckle, Cathy Ford, Mona Fertig, Peter Haase, On the Road for Poetry send-off party

For a few good years you gave us what every city needs, an informal place where writers can meet, read little mags, chapbooks and the latest award winning products, have coffee and be generally irreverent about what they have just read. Writers are less well served in space than are other artforms, given to fly-by-nite readings in coffee shops at the slack end of the week. We need lit storefronts, supported by the universities who see most of the money in the lit trade [mainly] squeezed from the bodies of long dead writers.[125]

On the Road for Poetry

The cross-country reading tour that Fertig had spoken of started with a bang on March 4. Both Fertig (*Mouth for Music*) and Cathy Ford (*the murdered dreams awake*) had new books out from Caitlin Press and were taking them to the streets, continent-wide. For Fertig, it meant leaving behind the centre she'd created for a while. She promised to report on the tour, on her return. The Storefront was the scene of their champagne kickoff reading for the thirty-four-day tour titled On the Road for Poetry, which would take them from Vancouver to New York. Admission was advertised as a bottle of champagne between two people, and attendees were encouraged to bring eats. This was the second trip for the pair. The first had been in 1979 when they'd read and toured seven cities in two weeks. Even though they had organized and negotiated the upcoming itinerary for months between them, their typical CanLit reading and billeting-with-the-locals tour strategy left plenty of room for improvisation, and at this late date, they were still hustling potential reading venues, particularly on the Prairies. Tour stops included Nelson, Edmonton, Saskatoon, Regina, Winnipeg, North Bay, Toronto, London, Kingston, Ottawa, St. John's, Charlottetown, Halifax and the Big Apple, New York.

How did a pair of broke, virtually unknown poets manage a coast-to-coast tour of a country the size of Canada? In those heady days, the Canada Council would fund author tours, organized by authors, and not just institutions or bookstores or galleries. If three to five readings could be arranged, travel and reading fees would be paid. Networking certainly helped. It was an ambitious undertaking. Fertig's subsequent published account reads:

On the road for poetry! Vancouver to Newfoundland to New York City. 17 cities in 5 weeks. After months and months of planning and letter writing and poster-making we're off. A great champagne kick-off at the Literary Storefront. 20-25 bottles popping. 50 people. Friends and beautiful rented glasses and an introduction we have to live up to. A purple beaded dress and a red velvet suit. We dress with energy.[126]

Cathy Ford writes:

Our tactic was to share our reading allotment through the Canada Council readings program ... Mona and I each had eight readings. If we shared, that meant we each had sixteen half-readings, and we plotted our way across Canada aiming for the mecca of New York to finish up our literary adventure. Mainly, I think, there were other poets and readings organizers, who were charmed by our sheer spunk. When people and bookstores we staked out to visit told us, "you know, poetry doesn't sell," we showed them our books, and usually, left a few behind, sometimes on consignment. But they were planted across the country. We learned that in this vast country the only way to find out about each other's work was to travel in person.[127]

In the Maritimes, they met up with Penn Kemp and became Three Voices, rehearsing reading and weaving the strands of their poems together in Charlottetown, Halifax and New York.

As the chapbook of a long Canadian reading tour, Fertig's collection *On the Road for Poetry: A Tour Journal* is as honest as it comes[128]—too much wine, lumpy couches, great dinners, bad dinners, selling books here and there, loneliness, frayed nerves, seal flippers for sale in St. John's, then news that President Reagan has just been shot. For the love and madness of poetry, they pressed on, selling books and post-cards en route. In the Big Apple, they lugged their cases up six flights of stairs in the Village, bought signed books by Patti Smith, visited galleries, viewed exhibitions of work by Gauguin and William Blake, took a walking pilgrimage through Central Park in homage to John Lennon at Strawberry Fields across from the Dakota and read at a Poetry Project session at St Mark's in the Bowery.

And at last they met Frances Steloff at the Gotham Book Mart— "Wise Men Fish Here." Fertig had yearned to meet the elderly Steloff before she died. On meeting the tiny legendary Steloff, Mona observed that "she had beautiful intense blue eyes just like Sheila Watson. She was one of my heroes." On April 10, they landed back on the shores of the Pacific, exhausted and happy.

Given its precarious financial position, almost unaccountably the Storefront was entering its fourth year in May. A gala party was orga-nized in honour of this unlikely survival story, and during National Book Festival week, a big night of readings and blarney hit Gastown on May 14, 8 PM. Headliners included Sharon Thesen, Keith Maillard, Ann York, Peter Trower, Joan Haggerty and performance poet Cat

Majors. With refreshments and a cash bar, the revels continued late after midnight.

Business carried on, sometimes with a wacky new spin. In June volunteers for a Wednesday evening newsletter mail-out session that usually featured beer were recruited with a fresh spiritual line: "Come share in the joyous dharma of the folding and unfolding of the universe. Experience the oneness of the all with the one. Help in this vital and uplifting task."

August floated in like a butterfly, with further liberating information that the City of Vancouver had awarded the Storefront $1,500 for operating expenses—enough to cover rent and a few bills. Another grant application had been directed to the Vancouver Foundation. Meanwhile, Leona Gom, a friend of the Storefront, earned $1,000 by winning the 1981 Canadian Authors Association Award for the best book of poetry, *Land of The Peace*.

Summer readers featured bill bissett reading from his new *Selected Poems: Beyond Even Faithful Legends*, Penn Kemp in from Ontario and Maxine Gadd over from Galiano Island for a Canada Council-sponsored "collaborative soundscape." Kemp, who read with Gadd, was "enthralled" by Gadd's poetic voice, as she was by Daphne Marlatt's for its "sonorous west coast sea swell . . . with all its resonant modulations."[129] She concluded, "The Literary Storefront is such a medium for growing Poetry, a rich and fertile seedbed very unlike the crisp, sharp-edged Toronto scene.[130]

Gadd's book of selected poems, *Lost Language*, edited by Daphne Marlatt and Ingrid Klassen, was in the process of being published by Coach House Press in Toronto. To take the pressure off while doing the edits, she stayed over at the Storefront, sleeping on the big couch. Ironically, one night, instead of being blissfully silent, the phone rang, "and a woman's voice ranted on as if into eternity."[131]

The 1981 fall calendar of events offered a promising cascade of readings and visits. On September 26, Joy Kogawa presented a Saturday

Clockwise from top left:
bill bissett, Mona Fertig, Susie Whiten
K.O. Kanne, Maxine Gadd, Cat Majors
Five Women Reading: Mona Fertig, Cat Majors, Cathy Ford, Dona Sturmanis
(Maxine Gadd behind Mona)

Ann York

Sharon Thesen

Helene Rosenthal
Photographs by Milton Bingham

night reading from her debut novel *Obasan*, which has since become a Canadian and North American classic. The poetic novel recounts the trials of Vancouver's Japanese Canadians during World War II, many of whom had lived an eight-minute walk up Powell Street. Born in Vancouver but living in Toronto, Kogawa had previously published several books of poetry, notably *Jericho Road*. Her visit, as a member of the League of Canadian Poets, was another Canada Council-sponsored hit.

Kogawa's appearance was followed soon after by Hungarian poet and political rebel George Faludy. Living in Toronto as an exile from the Communist regime, which he bitterly opposed after having endured its worst deprivations in the Recsk concentration camp, and prior to that as a Jew having escaped the Nazis by a whisker, Faludy brought a different kind of symbolism to poetry. A fiercely loveable poet, tragedy seemed to hang from him. For whatever reason, Faludy was the only visiting author the underfunded Storefront ever booked into a paid hotel room. Writers typically stayed with friends in town or were billeted.

What was inspiring was the number of events now being co-sponsored by other literary organizations. The Canada Council had the Storefront underlined in red as a reliable, well-organized venue for touring Canuck authors.[xiii]

Other shows were also routinely being fronted by Dallas Peterson, The Writers' Union, the League of Canadian Poets, and UBC's Department of Creative Writing journal, *Prism International*. This took organizational heat off Fertig and the Storefront volunteers. It kept the mix lively, unpredictable, and no one genre dominated.

---

xiii   The fall book season saw appearances from authors Robert Tyhurst, Richard Truhlar, Steve Smith, Bruce Robinson, Randy David, John Smith, David Frith, Joe Martin, Glen Sorestad, Colin Morton, Mary Di Michele, Jacqueline D'Amboise, Carolyn Zonailo, Beth Jankola, Elizabeth Gourlay, San Francisco's Gene Dennis, Sandy Shreve, Erin Mouré, Ted Laturnus, Mark Warrior, Genni Gunn and Rose Marie Tremblay, Bronwen Wallace, Ernest Hekkanen, Larry Geiler and Richard Payne.

It could get funky, even a bit weird, but if *Prism* wanted to have a special Halloween extravaganza with readers, singing and theatrical performances—especially if surrealism, mysticism and political satire were part of the stew—why not? Students produced other ambient events. Diana Hayes, poetry editor of *Prism*, read an erotic short story in a multi-media performance as part of her UBC graduate studies program in Creative Writing, while Alana Doyle, a BFA student in Fine and Performing Arts at SFU, danced behind a candle-lit scrim as recorded sounds of humpback whales were played. These events were well-attended by fellow MFA students who, as part of their graduating program, were expected to perform in public. Hayes' fellow students included Theresa Kishkan, Bill Gaston and Joan McLeod—all went on to successful literary careers. Her advisor was George McWhirter, and her fiction advisor was Robert Harlow; both were solid supporters of the Literary Storefront and read there themselves.[132]

In October Mona applied to the BC Cultural Fund for the second time, for an amount of $10,000, but this time it was not a joint application. In her application, she noted that government grants received between January 1 and the end of September of 1981 totalled $8,077. Membership income was $1,423, and as the books prepared by Linda Messmer indicated, there was a net loss on the year of $388.34. The Literary Storefront wasn't doing badly, but there was still no administrative money available beyond a small honorarium for the increasingly heavily used centre. Mona announced to the troops, "This year the Literary Storefront is applying for funding on its own as B.C.'s literary centre. The Writers' Union has applied separately [for their own program] . . . and the League of Poets feel they have not yet generated enough momentum to rightly join us this year."

The funds requested were to increase public awareness of the Storefront's own purpose, services and events. Her application continued: "In the future the development of the B.C. Writers Federation should help us collectively work towards common concerns and goals such as the importance of the literary arts in this province. So, at present, the Literary Storefront constitutes a stable, physical nerve centre for the B.C. literary arts . . . We invite you to visit us in the future." [133]

But things could, and sometimes did, slip. The previous year's Fall Equinox Festival, for example, had been a critical and creative success that raised the general consciousness of Vancouver considerably; the downside was that when the accounts were all adjusted, there was a deficit of $400. These were early 1980s' dollars, real money. It was time again, Fertig called, for members and supporters to dig deep. So life slid up and down the financial razor blade. Newsletter mail-outs and volunteer hoots could be fun—"join us for a liquid lunch, stamping, stapling and mailing out the great news carrier."

And the world could still turn blue on a dime. If the November 1981 events sheet of issue #42 looked thin, indeed it was. As a banner line admitted, "Sorry! The Literary Storefront Newsletter is out of production due to lack of an Editor! We are able to bring you only the Storefront's Events. If you can help, please call us!"

In a satiric send-up that might have had George Faludy knotting his spectacularly bushy eyebrows in worry, that same November, the Storefront and The Writers' Union would offer a workshop on How to Write a Successful Romantic Novel for Harlequin Books, led by Irene Robertson. Then the annual general meeting on November 29 gave everyone a turn at setting the world to rights. "Come one, come all!" the announcement read. "The Literary Storefront NEEDS YOU, NEEDS YOU, NEEDS YOU."

After the AGM, December's miraculously, partially restored newsletter confessed to ongoing organizational difficulties:

Enclosed in this partial newsletter are the minutes of our fairly successful 2nd Annual General Meeting. From this you should be able to get a good idea of our present situation. We have voted to hold an Extraordinary Annual General Meeting Feb.21.82 to decide how committees have been working and what our financial situation is.

Our main problem is structure. No one person should be handling everything and when a volunteer hasn't been able to complete a job the task falls to the core person to pick it up. As a result, in the past few months we have had a lot of difficulties. Communication has broken down. Workshops were cancelled. The October calendar didn't get sent to the media, libraries, etc, and as a result we had very poor attendance for Oct. events. The newsletter has been full of spelling mistakes and errors of dates and omission of certain important details. There was no editor for November as the core person decided not to pick up the pieces, again. So, until the present new committees are in working order and we have found an events committee there will be no further readings. No Open Reading for December. In January, with the help of a few volunteers we will try to maintain one day a week where we are open to the public. During this time mail and phone calls will be answered. But don't ask for info in a hurry. The Writers' Union will continue its regular hours and Dallas Peterson & Co. are in and out most of the week. The vision of the Storefront is to provide a place/space for all writers and groups to communicate, interact, and to promote the growth of the literary arts on the West Coast. An Aquarian ideal. All things are possible. So hopefully we are on to a brighter course. With a lot of changes. The volunteer form enclosed is for you to fill out and return by the end of December. In the future we will also open the newsletter to monthly guest editorials so if you have something to say, write the Publications Committee. We are also asking those with OVERDUE MEMBERSHIPS TO PLEASE RENEW. Our printing bill is the largest and only memberships can help us through the winter months. BUY A FRIEND ONE FOR CHRISTMAS! Donations are tax deductible. There will also be a small increase of membership fees due to the drastic increase of postage . . . Membership is now $17/year.[134]

Literary Storefront, #1-314 W. Cordova St

1982: Exhaustion, Excitement and Existential Thistles

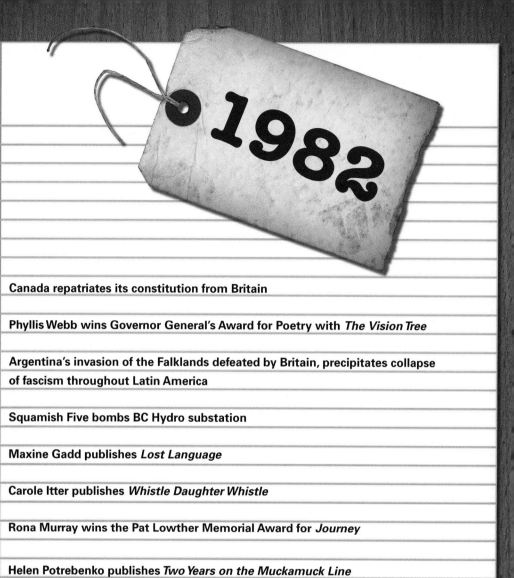

1982

Canada repatriates its constitution from Britain

Phyllis Webb wins Governor General's Award for Poetry with *The Vision Tree*

Argentina's invasion of the Falklands defeated by Britain, precipitates collapse of fascism throughout Latin America

Squamish Five bombs BC Hydro substation

Maxine Gadd publishes *Lost Language*

Carole Itter publishes *Whistle Daughter Whistle*

Rona Murray wins the Pat Lowther Memorial Award for *Journey*

Helen Potrebenko publishes *Two Years on the Muckamuck Line*

Vancouver declares itself a nuclear-free zone

Construction begins on the Expo 86 site.

Joe Fortes Branch of the Vancouver Public Library, named for the beloved English Bay lifeguard, opens on Denman Street

CBC produces *Between the Sky and the Splinters*, a film portrait of poet Peter Trower

George Fertig

Nineteen eighty-two rolled forward on the calendar. No one knew it would be a watershed year. An application to Canada Council for funding support for the newsletter was not successful. Instead, there was hope of support from the City of Vancouver and the BC Cultural Fund.

A St. Valentine's Day Dance of the Heart and literary event was planned with music by Ian Ayre McConkey and the Accousticats, from the popular Soft Rock Café on 4th Avenue. A belly dancer—a phenomenon still relatively new to town—would perform the body language of love, and between sets, a slate of readers gave five-minute readings of love poetry.

On February 12, the landlord unexpectedly sent a letter saying,

"Dancing was not permitted on the premises" and that the Valentine's event should be cancelled because the 100-year-old building's floor could not take it. Evelyn Fertig, still one of the desk volunteers, wrote back, "too late to cancel."

New energy kicked in. After the extraordinary annual general meeting in February, Tom Ilves, an urbane volunteer from the U.S. east coast whose wife taught at UBC, began a series of Author Nights focusing on the analysis and discussion of certain authors' work, beginning with a presentation on the fiction of Thomas Pynchon. Other new volunteer names and faces surfaced, several of which would become steadily more prominent, notably Wayne Holder from the Fraser Valley, who also had friends and faculty connections at UBC and was from the U.S.

On February 23, 1982, Tom Fielding of the BC Cultural Fund wrote Fertig, "It was a recommendation of the Board that a decision on your application be deferred pending further adjudication by the Literary Advisory Committee . . . it will be considered at its April meeting . . . please accept my apologies for this delay and I hope it will not seriously inconvenience your organization."

The Storefront's horizon looked upbeat and promising. No one expected what was coming next.

The March newsletter included a bombshell editorial by Dona Sturmanis which read:

As of April 1, Mona Fertig, Founder and Director of the Literary Storefront, will be departing to Montreal for an extended leave of absence to pursue her own blossoming poetic career, and take a well-deserved vacation from her duties here for almost four years. Mona has done a magnificent job of creating and developing Western Canada's only literary centre. We owe it to her to continue building the Literary Storefront.

The present administration is now in the hands of committees, consisting of members of our non-profit society. Though philosophically appealing, decentralization has its disadvantages, primarily lack of focus and communication. It will take a special effort to maintain effective decision making this way; this could be accomplished in the following manner:

a) More communication between people at the Storefront on a day-to-day basis, and the various committees, many members of whom only visit the premises at their appointed meeting times and for special events.

As well as handling calls, visitors, events set-up and cleaning up, Ingrid Klassen of The Writers' Union and the folks in the back office (Dallas Peterson Associates) have often helped handle Storefront operational problems that could only be dealt with at the moment, rather than through a volunteer or a committee. This is supplemental, of course, to the excellent job volunteers have done running the Storefront from 1-5 PM during the week, and the efforts individual committee members have put forward to organize events. (We all know about the Valentine's Dance . . . much thanks to Claudia, Gordon, Peter, Jennifer, and Evelyn, and those who worked hard.)

b) Grant money needs to be found to hire one person to assume responsibility for routine administration of the Storefront, answering to all committees. This would serve to make the jobs and functions of all committees more effective.

We also do not have the profile in the literary scene that we deserve, because of lack of an organized image. This is partially due to the current shift in administration structure, and resulting ambiguity in events and fund-raising decisions.

Our surroundings could also be improved. We need sprucing up. Paint is only a beginning. It has perennially been left to a handful of people to even maintain a presentable environment—i.e., watering plants, washing coffee cups, straightening papers, emptying garbage, buying supplies, vacuuming, and sweeping the stairs. As members of the Storefront, we should all be taking much more pride in our

Mona and Sylvia
Photograph by
Milton Bingham

surroundings, both for our own use and that of the general public. More input from members, in the way of suggestions, and active participation is necessary.

Finally, I must bring up the subject of money. The Literary Storefront operates with the help of grants, memberships, and donations. When the grants do not come through, we must use our own ideas to raise more money to meet costs of rent, newsletter printing, and other expenses. Since we are set up to act as a service for the public, a writer's centre, there should be more interest from our members as to how we can raise money. Please call us or write with suggestions. Also tell us how we can help you as a writer.

Send more donations. Be financially generous at our events. Rent our space for $30 a night. Come in and buy books at our bookstore. Get a friend to become a member. Buy a Lottery Ticket at $1 a piece (chance at $100; draw on March 15).If you regularly come to the Open Readings, I suggest you donate two dollars to help us. There are at least fifteen of you who show up every month.

Please become more involved in supporting the Storefront. Our existence depends on your interest.

And please come to our send-off party for Mona on March 27 at 8 PM so when she goes off to Montreal, she will rest assured the Storefront is doing just fine.[135]

It was the end of an era. Mona was leaving town, leaving the Storefront that she'd created and nurtured. As she explained many years later:

By the fourth year of running the Literary Storefront full-time, I was exhausted. The struggle to find funding and volunteers was constant. I was also writing and publishing and had crossed Canada twice on two reading tours. So, with great regret, I decided it was time for me to leave the Storefront and let the members take over. If the Storefront was an entity that could stand on its two feet without me, then I hoped I had done my job.

Storefront supporters and regulars hadn't realized how rundown Fertig had become in keeping the whole organization and centre afloat. On arriving in Montreal the following month, she applied for welfare. When she explained her psychological and physical fatigue and told them that temporarily she couldn't work, they gave her assistance forthwith.

Feeling the jitters, on March 1, a month before Mona left, Dona Sturmanis of Dallas Peterson Associates wrote Mona to formalize her tenancy, pointing out:

Trevor Carolan, David Watmough, Classical Joint, Photograph by Margrith Schraner

In the event The Writers' Union cannot rent the office across the hall for April I would like to rent it. If the BC Federation of Writers wants to rent it later, we will give it back to them, or they can rent part of the front space. You can count on me for this. Also can you write a letter of consent, authorizing that I can stay on renting here as your lessee, just in case when the Federation moves in, or strange things happen with the autocracy of the Literary Storefront, I have your permission and authorization to stay on here. One never knows what can happen, and I do not want to be suddenly uprooted, cuz I really like it here![136]

In telegraphing new directions, the March newsletter also noted that eminent English poet and man of letters Stephen Spender would be reading at the Literary Storefront on April 6. Spender's career had already spanned five decades, and his speaking tours were an opportunity to hear stories first-hand about many of the twentieth century's critical literary developments.

Then before what would be a watershed date in Storefront history, on March 20, the Federation of British Columbia Writers held its inaugural AGM at Langara College after eighteen months of meetings, often at the Storefront, with representatives of all major professional writers' organizations. The new executive council was: Chairman, David Watmough; 1st Vice, James Barber and 2nd Vice, K.O. Kanne. Council comprised Carolyn Zonailo, Tom Wayman, Fred Wah, Michael Mercer, Chris Moore, Christie Harris, John Lent and Daniel Wood. The Membership Committee was George Payerle, Irene Robertson, Richard Payne, Leona Gom and Jan Drabek.[137]

At the AGM, which Fertig and Fielding attended, Fielding publicly recognized the Literary Storefront as an important group that the new Federation must work with. Mona knew this was a pivotal moment, one that had taken many years to arrive, and she was elated that it had come before she had left. On March 30, Fertig wrote to Fielding:

It was great to be recognized at the Writers' Federation as a valuable organization! I hope the Arts Board will agree and we will hear soon about our application. Everything is finally coming together after four years of very hard work. You will see in our next newsletter our ideas on association with them, which you helped clarify for me. The Storefront's Board and their executive will meet next week with Stephen Spender to talk about future plans etc. It makes more sense [for the two organizations] to apply separately for funding. The main people who will [now] be looking after the Storefront are Tom Ilves, Dona Sturmanis, Randy Maxted, Wayne Holder and three committees and a Board. Our policy has not changed only the way things are run . . . I leave April 10 for six months in Montreal. To write, read, rest and reflect. But I will be back.[138]

Fertig also reported on the business of the meeting:

[It] was very chaotic and distressing in the morning with every-one arguing about memberships. There is a real split about an open Federation or a closed one for professionals. But after the lunch hour meeting, things became calm, even tranquil, especially since we re-alized once Tom Fielding spoke, that the gov. is who we have to communicate with and convince, and that is where we should be directing our energies. Not [fighting] amongst ourselves.[139]

For the Literary Storefront's hundreds of members who had come to depend on Fertig's passion and energy, the possibility of an alterna-tive future was unsettling. No one knew what the next step forward might look like, or how it would unfold. With Fertig's departure imminent, Cat Majors saw directly what the Storefront's community had been given, and that was now vulnerable:

The Literary Storefront Days in the early 'Eighties were like something straight out of the kind of bohemia that one can only imagine must have surrounded the Beat Generation... a low budget, high energy blast of an upstairs underground happening pad with an on-the-edge twist... It provided a much needed and fertile com-bination testing ground and home base for baby wayward poets to find themselves and for the experienced literati to turn up sometimes unexpectedly in an aura of excitement... a stimulating cauldron of poetry and performance that would sizzle and crackle sometimes long into the night. Definitely the closest thing we had to a Paris boîte, a San Francisco Speakeasy or a Cosmic New York Café.[140]

Maxine Gadd would echo Majors' affection and concern:

The Literary Storefront was both warm and cool, elevated above Cordova St. when this route out of town was, as it always is, changing its small commercial models on the street front but not yet the social centre for the brilliantly beautiful young from the suburbs that it often is today . . . at night it was lofty over the dark and quiet unless the poetry parties were encamped by Mona and Peter to up and astound the local ghosts, who were always wandering about for a good time, as in any ancient part of the city of the world . . . Always after Literary wonders were conviviality, food and drink and music and dance. As if in the court of Eleanor of Aquitaine.[141]

As Peter said years later, "It came to an end for her in 1982 when she got totally burned out. The American lads, Tom and Wayne, took over then, but no one had the hands for it all like Mona. She was the mother of all that."[142]

Fertig handed over the reins to the Storefront committees, including the board of directors that consisted of Gordon Cornwall, Jennifer Alley, Cathy Ford, Dona Sturmanis, ElJean Wilson, and Tom Ilves. Ingrid Klassen of TWUC and the Dallas Peterson Associates would also be helping with maintenance functions. At a bittersweet farewell party, she was presented with a red rose, one at a time, throughout the night, and Peter gave her a blue trunk to pack her things in. She recalls:

> I was going to Montreal to live with my sister. To recuperate, to do nothing, to throw away my watch and calendar. To maybe write. Peter and I agreed to separate, which was very painful, but somehow I could not think about what the future held and knew I just needed rest and time alone. He would go to Australia and we would stay in touch . . . Once I'd made this decision I began the process, and it took months of turning everything over to committees and the Board of Directors. It was an enormous task. On the day I left, on the way to the airport, I realized I'd forgotten to take my typewriter and we had to turn back to get it. It was a sad time for both of us. I now entered a period of unprecedented uncertainty. As Rilke said, "be patient toward all that is unsolved in your heart and try to love the questions themselves." From this, several years later, my book of dreams, drawings and poems, *4722 Rue Berri*, was published.[143]

There was nervousness at her departure. "What I remember is Mona's personality, her enthusiasm. But by the time she left, she was exhausted," ElJean Wilson recalls. "During her time there it was free, hospitable. I think she was better organized than it appeared. There was cohesiveness at the Literary Storefront that she knit together, and she just knew so many people."[144] Confirming Wilson's position, Ingrid Klassen adds, "She needed to get away. It gave her some perspective when she left that there wasn't anything else she could do, and the Storefront seemed to carry on fine for awhile after that."[145]

Fertig wrote a last letter urging the board to provide at least a two-month guarantee of tenancy to Dona Sturmanis.[146]

Cathy Ford recounts her uncertainty of the changes:

Everyone was getting worn . . . When Mona went to Montreal, and the new board came in, I was already concerned about the direction things might go, and only re-committed to help keep the faith. I had limited input as I was travelling from Mayne, and working mostly on the newsletter, trying to keep the communications lines going. Although the women in the back offices were still doing it, in terms of the day-to-day work of the Storefront and its aims, there was already the front edge of a power struggle... There was of course, some support for perceived new energy, like bright new pennies, lying about with access to the famous, and the funds to bring them in. The burgeoning economic shortfall convinced me that I too needed a rest . . . Perhaps I was out of step. Perhaps I needed to contribute in a more positive way to something else, loop out for a while.[147]

April's newsletter broadcasted energy. It featured news of an evolving Seattle connection. A report explained that contacts had been established with the literary community in Seattle when Randy Maxted and new writers Wayne Holder and Tom Ilves, now members of the programme committee, had driven down to meet with representatives of the Poetry Exchange, the Red Sky Reading Series and a liaison group from the Emerald City's annual end-of-summer Bumbershoot Arts Festival. Henceforward, newsletters would be exchanged between Seattle's Poetry Exchange and the Storefront. The Storefront's monthly edition would now be available at several bookstores in the Seattle area. In pre-Internet days, this was highly useful news for writers and anyone planning publicity for a book or arts project. Other than Victoria, Seattle was the only city within reasonable driving distance from Vancouver; a couple of hours to the south, it offered an opportunity for Storefront members and sympathizers to network, read and unofficially shop their wares in an important U.S. hub.

A reading exchange of poets was also being lined up for July: five poets from Vancouver would be invited to present two readings and appear on KRAB radio, and the following week, the Storefront would reciprocate in hosting a similar contingent from Seattle with readings on Cordova Street and on CFRO. Adding to developments was word of a co-operative effort to bring literary readers to western Canada and the northwest U.S. This would potentially reduce the costs of presenting headliner readers from out of town.

Change continued to shake the buds of spring. Not only did Fertig leave, but so did The Writers' Union of Canada and the League of Canadian Poets. The Writers' Union had not received hoped for funding from the BC Cultural Fund and terminated their tenancy April 1, writing that this was due to "total lack of funds now and in the months to come. It is with regret that we end our tenancy association."[148] The League of Canadian Poets no longer had the volunteers or the finances.

Sturmanis did take over both back offices for Dallas Peterson Associates paying $130 a month. Their tenure would become worthy of note among literary history buffs for the presence of the precociously talented young worker who'd join them.

Ironically, after Mona flew off, the BC Cultural Fund mailed a letter on April 14, 1982, stating, "I am pleased to advise you that a project grant of $6,000 has been awarded to assist in costs associated with the Literary Storefront and the production of its newsletter. Best wishes for a successful year." Mona heard about the grant's success after she'd landed in Montreal.

Stephen Spender Pays a Call

An Evening with Stephen Spender

Sponsored by the Vancouver Poetry
Festival Society

British Poetry Social at the
Literary Storefront

Featuring reminiscences of
W.H. Auden, T.S. Eliot, C. Day Lewis,
Christopher Isherwood, The Bloomsbury Circle et al

Questions and discussion to follow
**Tuesday, April 6, 8:00 p.m.
at the Literary Storefront
1-314 West Cordova, Vancouver**

$5.00 at the door
Cash bar.
All proceeds to the Literary Storefront.

A lot of Storefront regulars had come to think of the Storefront as a drop-in home. Now Fertig was gone "on extended leave," but the centre would carry on. Bill Jeffries remembers how "in the '80s at Cordova there were a lot of ashtrays, a lot of smoke and gnomes working away at unknown projects in the back room—like Doug Coupland, when he was still a student at Vancouver School of Art."[149]

Coupland, who would eventually land his colossal hit novel *Generation X*, would remember the Literary Storefront astutely and with affection:

I did paste-up and layout for Erik Nordholm and Dona Sturmanis who had the rooms in the back, a lovely job I look back on fondly. It was in the middle of my art school years, 1982 & 1983 and Wayne Holder, Hildi and Tom Ilves (currently King of Estonia or something equally unexpected) were the people I knew . . . My light table was eight feet away from the lectern and mike, and I got to attend every poetry reading there for free. Some nights, when there were no attendees, I was drafted to fill up a chair in the audience. I remember there were some writing groups that met once a week. Everybody was thoroughly nuts but in a charming way . . . I went to maybe two of them before everybody's ego made me flee. I've no idea about the Storefront's politics . . . I was too young and clueless to pay any attention, but I remember money was always a huge issue. And they had a terrific collection of small press books and poetry. Did they get saved? Even then they seemed ephemeral and easily lost.[150]

Days before Mona departed, Stephen Spender arrived in Vancouver on April 6. The Storefront's new day-to-day operators invited reps of various literary organizations to a private dinner with Spender at the Nairobi, an East African restaurant around the corner from the Storefront. Among the attendees were David Watmough and James Barber of Urban Peasant foodie program fame, and as one of the invitees, I recall a dramatic moment arising when, at odds with the two over the Argentine military government's invasion of the Falkland Islands only four days before, in defence of Britain's preparing to hammer the Argentines in retaliation, Spender slammed the table declaring, "I won't stand for jackboot fascism!"

Spender brought glamour to the Storefront with his recollections of Pound, Eliot, H.D. and London's great modernist and imagist poets. It was a sweltering evening. Vancouver artist Jack Shadbolt sat prominently near the front, engrossed in Spender's stories. In a private word with him later, Shadbolt confessed to sharing youthful political justice ideals with the leftist Auden gang in which Spender was a central figure. Spender was generous in making space for others from the audience and, in the old Storefront tradition, signed many books before departing wearily for his hotel.

In a review of Spender, poet Randolph Maxted commented,

He treated those of us . . . about 150 souls within bursting walls, to a taste of one of the most prolific literary liaisons in history, Bloomsbury: Lady Ottoline Morrell, superlative hostess; Yeats, superlative enigma; Woolf, vulnerable, defensive; Eliot, polite, compassionate. No less scintillating were his harkenings to friendship with Auden and Isherwood, "pansy leftists" vilified by Orwell who, upon meeting Spender regretted not seeing the apple for the bushel. Spender loves to namedrop. That's what we want, says he. He's seventy-three. If you squint, he looks like Robert Frost . . . I see how beautiful, intelligent, he is, how little my own age, as I ask for an autograph. [151]

Spender himself was more circumspect. In his *Journals 1939-1983*, he acknowledges having dinner with Wayne Holder and his wife Hildi Adelhelm, and with poet Robert Bringhurst. Reading Bringhurst's poetry the next morning, he says: "[I was] bowled over. They were poems about ice and stone and light—of a dazzling purity—something so elusive and so controlled . . . showing the utter commonplaceness of the confessional writing fashionable now."[152]

Of his talk at the Storefront, he is not so flattering of the Vancouver audience. Sounding like a character from a Chekhov short story—the self-absorbed, visiting government official—he writes:

I was asked to reminisce about literary life. It was the excitement of provincials for whom I represented a world from which they felt cut off . . . There was a kind of excitement which, with some of the young, was erotic in a platonic way . . . The crowd were anxious for every crumb of information I could give them about Sylvia Beach, Adrienne Monnier, etc. It was a strange evening.[153]

It was strange for Maxine Gadd as well, who writes, "I remember attending the exhausted and disdainful Stephen Spender, who really didn't like my query about past literary feuds."[154] To this David Watmough would add, "I also recall an angry Stephen Spender when, introducing him, I referred to the U.S. (anti-Cold War) origins of his literary magazine *Encounter* in which I happened to make my critical debut. We were never friends after that!"[155]

Spender did not forget his Vancouver visit though. At conferences and PEN festivals, the perennial globetrotter was kind to West Coast writers who mentioned his reading visit, and at one such occasion in Toronto, that I was part of some years later, he noted similarities between the situations of Canadian poets he'd met and that of his Auden gang and Bloomsbury friends in younger days when to sell several hundred copies of a new book was typical.[156] For Canadian and West Coast poets, book sales had not changed dramatically.

A month later, buoyed by BC Cultural funding and the Spender success, the Storefront began operating Mondays through Fridays, 10 AM to 5 PM. In a visible sign of energy, the newsletter had a new layout and was carefully proofread. On June 30, member Johann E. Polberg wrote complimenting the change: "The entire format is greatly improved and the new directions of the Storefront are given excellent coverage." Wayne Holder led an Author's Night discussion of Regionalism in the Work of U.S. Writers James Wright and Philip Levine—a remote subject for most Vancouver writers. Other such events were led by Andreas Schroeder on Jorge Luis Borges, and by Francesca Newton-Moss on A.E. Housman and Philip Larkin.

Programming was one thing. Critical day-to-day and substantive administrative decision-making were quite another. In a problematic letter that got to the heart of new and possible future trajectories concerning the Literary Storefront's direction and its ethical and financial accountability, board member Jennifer Alley, being unable to attend a meeting, wrote to her colleagues from Nevada. Congratulating the members on the success of the Spender evening, she had concerns about the amount being proposed for an upcoming Edward Albee Festival and felt the Storefront's aggregate debt should be served first. Similarly, she felt the main administrator [Tom Ilves] should indeed be paid, even a $300 per month stipend, but not contemplated "until all the Storefront's debts are paid, big ones and little personal ones—we also have an honorarium to give Mona for past inspiration and service of $500."[157] Since the BC Cultural grant was the only one to be used for administrative costs, she felt that basic rent costs and newsletter postage needed guaranteeing from the grant funding, as well as a small sum for paying "local Canadian poets."[158]

There was also the matter of an actual job description for the executive director. "This would help us in grant applications later," Alley continued:

I would like Tom, if the job is created as we wish, to train another person on that job as well. There was, Mona found, a tendency for people to dump work on the director and for Committees to rely too much on her/him, and that resulted in burn out. Should it do so for Tom he could take a break by transferring the job to the second person, and should he leave, the second person could carry it on.[159]

Jennifer Alley

Tom Ilves, Mona Fertig,
Photograph by Brian Kent/*Vancouver Sun*

8

Turning Point: Tom Ilves and Wayne Holder

From a Vancouver perspective, Tom Ilves was a quintessential Ivy League man looking for a gig, a place to fit in—freelance editing, publishing, teaching.

As a freelance journalist, I became acquainted with Ilves in 1982 when I needed to rent a space for several Saturday morning seminars that PWAC was running. After a stunningly successful PWAC event organized at the Planetarium with Priscilla Flood, the executive editor of *Esquire* magazine from New York, and local syndicated political columnist Allen Fotheringham, it seemed a good idea to host a follow-up event with Edith Iglauer, the fine nature writer who had married a fisherman from Pender Harbour and wrote for the *New Yorker*. Alan Twigg and David Watmough agreed to join Iglauer in addressing the transition from journalism to book-writing. We needed a location like the Storefront.

It was the age of typewriters, but writers were starting to hear of computers, so we first organized a learning session and invited some of the city's early commercial computer specialists to a session on technology as well. That led to a PWAC seminar on Scriptwriting for Television with Michael Mercer from ACTRA, Richard Paluck and Tony Robertson. The Storefront was a perfect location, and we organized the panel discussions along similar lines to the regular events, with tickets at $3 and $4.

My conversation with Ilves and his friend Wayne Holder turned to West Coast U.S. writers. I'd studied at Humboldt State in California, and my time there had dovetailed with Ray Carver's in the nearby Redwoods area. His first major prose collection, *Will You Please Be Quiet, Please?*, had just come out, and his closest friend, Dick Day, was a professor I'd known. Carver's brilliant "Cathedral" period stories revolutionized American short story writing, and I shared Tom's and Wayne's intrigue with Carver's facility in working with both prose fiction and poetry, and his working class perspectives. Ilves was interested that, prior to my mid-'70s in the U.S., I had also journeyed a number of times to communist Eastern Europe—a place rarely visited by Westerners then, and a time now generally regarded there and in Russia as "the Period of Stagnation."

Tom was born in Sweden to an émigré Estonian family, raised in New Jersey and had attended Columbia University in New York. Whether it was that I'd travelled behind the Iron Curtain or that I'd written letters to Eastern Bloc governments in support of jailed writers, we shared a number of sympathies and began knocking about Vancouver together. Holder and Ilves knew Jack Foster, an Irish professor teaching literature at UBC, and invited me out there several times to meet various scholars. They'd bring Foster to the Storefront for a Dublin-style literary "Bloomsday" bash in summer that celebrated James Joyce and his remarkable association with Sylvia Beach of the original Shakespeare and Company. In this process, I could see that while Tom had a broad knowledge of U.S. writers and writing, his familiarity with Vancouver's literary history was limited. No surprise there, but he had a talent for synthesizing and summarizing the writers and their work that he encountered, a useful skill for a future political leader. We'd hang around the waterfront and some of the East Van dives I knew that journalists frequented. He was fascinated. Tom was always urbane—good tweed jacket, always a sweater over a tie or dickie, good shoes, bookish with clipped hair. A brainy, well-read kind of guy, with a master's in psychology, though a little bashful. He said that he did editing work for faculty types at UBC. "Atrocious writers, the academics," he claimed — and in need of work, I noted this. You'd see a copy of the *New York Times* tucked under his arm. None of the local grinders could afford it; we'd be carrying the *Vancouver Sun* or the *Georgia Straight*. Ilves' wife, Dr. Merry Bullock, was an assistant professor with the Department of Psychology at UBC, 1979-1984, and eventually became a leading figure in the American Psychology Association. Before he left Vancouver, Ilves himself taught as well in Estonian literature and linguistics for a year at Simon Fraser University.

It was never exactly clear when Tom and Wayne arose in the Storefront's community. They evolved as volunteers early in 1982 on the programme committee, then within a relatively short time, when no one else took up the reins, became the Storefront's management by default. During their tenure at the helm, they brought pizzazz to Vancouver's literary agenda, and they received plenty of encouragement for their events, although to outsiders the sources of their funding were cloudy. But ultimately, as exciting as the events they planned were, their creative direction was not without friction, and the level of programming they envisioned proved financially unsustainable.

Wayne Holder and Hildi Adelhelm lived in Mission, where they owned a successful land title search firm and maintained a literary salon at their home on Clay Road. Holder collected books, many signed, and it was at his home that I first saw an original edition of Jack Kerouac's *On the Road*. He served on the executive council of the Federation of BC Writers in 1983-84, and it was through this association that my wife, Kwangshik and I met poets like Crispin Elsted, Robert Bringhurst, Marion Quednau, George Payerle, and good translators like Riina Tamm. While Holder and Ilves did solid work bringing in ranking personalities to Vancouver, a persistent strain of anti-Americanism circulated during their tenure, and some moderate to hard-core leftists in Vancouver's literary community fretted that the Americans had subterranean affiliations.

There were a few ways to look at this situation. From the 1960s onward, Canadian culture had consciously struggled to establish itself as an independent entity separate from mother country British colonialism and constantly encroaching U.S. culture alike. Rightly, many in the arts and academic communities did not want to see this national growth undermined or usurped by U.S. influence especially. At the same time, as Bill Jeffries observed, an ironic hometown protectionism could also come "from people who thought the 1963 Poetry Conference at UBC was the best and most important thing that ever happened"—as if it was a landmark Canadian nationalist celebration.[162] This even though the great majority of headline writers had been American men with only two women invited—Margaret Avison and Denise Levertov. Downtown, logic tended to blur with emotion and politics.

In 1988, while coordinating a literary festival at the Calgary Olympic Winter Games, I encountered Wayne Holder again at a reception. Among the guests was Jaan Kaplinski, the Estonian poet who'd seen his share of political troubles under the Soviets. At the event I looked up to see Wayne Holder. Now living in the U.S., where he ran a book-shop in San Francisco, Wayne had journeyed north for the event. Like Ilves, he was an easy fellow to like.

Curiously, I helped make possible Tom Ilves' first visit to his ancestral homeland at age thirty-one, when he travelled with Wayne Holder to what was then the Soviet Union. They'd approached me early in 1984 with the idea of getting into the Soviet Union and travelling unhindered by the customary state apparatchiks. I'd just taken a job as editor with the *Vancouver Voice*, a new, soon-to-be short-lived weekly paper founded by the mercurial Dermot Travis. With offices in Gastown, like many such publishing projects, it began promisingly. After the first and only published edition that included a review of Thomas Pynchon by Ilves and a hip, quirky article by Douglas Coupland entitled "A Night at the Montgomery Café," Wayne and Tom approached me with the idea of writing dispatches from the Soviet Union, which they hoped to visit. A commissioning letter from me might make it easier for them to move about. I furnished them with letters for the Soviet embassy in Ottawa, and they set off. When the paper collapsed with speed shortly thereafter, amid the pandemonium of unpaid printer's bills, unhappy writers and myself unpaid, I wondered, what's come out of all this? Weirdly, two American writers were travelling in the Soviet Union with credentials I'd provided for them for a paper that no longer existed.

Wayne Holder, Crispen Elsted, Robert Bringhurst, Jaan Kaplinski in background, 1988, Olympic Literary Arts Festival, Photograph by Vincent J. Varga

Meanwhile readings at the Storefront in the spring of 1982 featured Eileen Kernaghan, Gordon Cornwall, Daphne Marlatt, Helen Potrebenko and Audrey Thomas. Gerry Gilbert called by to cap a long spring reading tour with his "Annual Report," a poetic occasion that *Province* arts reviewer Max Wyman singled out for its "unique ability to offend, amuse and move an audience." In an experimental bilingual reading, a rising young French-Canadian novelist, Charles-Auguste Lavoie, read in French with a translator. In September, Tom Ilves wrote to Lavoie:

We've been inspired to start a French Language series at the Storefront with Michel Beaulieu giving a reading next month. Otherwise the Storefront has become quite hectic again with two to four readings a week, some of them good, the others, well . . . I've been hiding out at home writing grants to keep the place going, editing silly books . . . eating, and occasionally, all too occasionally, I've been able to write a little fiction. Wayne, meanwhile is working hard on his poetry and meeting with some success. His first book just came out and by and large the response had been very positive, especially on the part of the better local poets.[163]

After writing a short review on Adrienne Rich for the newsletter, the redoubtable Jane Rule came down to Gastown once more to moderate a special panel discussion workshop titled The Politics of Content in Canadian Women's Writing. Also participating were Leona Gom, Joanne Hannah, bookseller Thora Howell, Nora Randall and Pat Smith. Two theatre-focused programs ran as well: a presentation of Anne Cameron's *Rites of Passage* and an evening with playwright Tom Cone, then revelling in hits at Stratford, New York and Chicago.

Music content comprised a benefit dance at Britannia School with the Moral Lepers and a songwriting workshop featuring the West Coast's always crowd-pleasing Shari Ulrich and Ferron. "Come early and stay late!" the advertising rang.

Thanks to an additional grant from the Leon and Thea Koerner Foundation, another creative series commenced when children's book authors Christie Harris and Ainsley Manson inaugurated a Sundays at the Storefront program for children. Scheduled for the last Sunday of each month at 2:30 PM, two children's book authors would read from recently published work. The afternoons were free to children, and cookies and punch were served. Manson read from her just-published West Vancouver-set work *Mr. McUmphrie of Caulfield Cove*. Claudia Cornwall served as contact person for the series.

Among the more intriguing productions was a Saturday London Fog Night fundraising dinner and get-acquainted party for Storefront members and supporters. Roast beef, Yorkshire pudding, scones and bar service were included for $15.

The buzz, however, was about two bigger, bolder names soon to descend. In June Czeslaw Milosz, Nobel Laureate for Literature in 1980, would read at John Oliver Secondary School in "one of the most important literary events of the year." For the city's Polish community, he promised to read a number of poems in his native language.

The much-ballyhooed appearance of Milosz came and went, but not as smoothly as expected. Holder offered a post-mortem in the newsletter:

The Milosz reading represented the climax of three months' work and preparation.

We would like to gratefully acknowledge the support and assistance of the Polish community of Vancouver in making his visit a relative success. This is the first time that the Literary Storefront has hosted the appearance of a Nobel Prize winner and that in itself makes it an historic event . . . I arrived at the airport just in time for the scheduled arrival of Mr. Milosz' flight in my best three-piece suit . . .

My great admiration for Mr. Milosz' poetry, which I know only in translation, and for his personal courage in his anti-fascist activities during World War II and in his opposition to the Soviet domination of Poland following the war, made it a moment of high anticipation for me. One of the few recompenses of organizing literary events is the opportunity to have some personal contact with people of Milosz' calibre.

He came off the plane in a tweed jacket and a Greek fisherman's cap, looking like an aging seaman. His eyebrows, each of which would make an admirable moustache for a lesser man, made him immediately recognizable. Also familiar was the stern expression that looks back at us on all of his photographs . . . Yes, he had seen Philip Levine recently, and yes, he remembered very well his conversations with William Everson, then Brother Antoninus, in the seminary in Oakland . . . He confirmed what I had heard elsewhere, that Kenneth Rexroth is desperately ill after his recent stroke and that he can speak only a few words.

We arrived at the CKVU studios to find a large crowd milling outside carrying signs and placards. For a moment I thought that the Marxist-Leninists had decided to arrange a reception, protesting the presence of the avowedly anti-Soviet Nobel Laureate. Fortunately, this was not the case. What we had encountered was a demonstration of student nurses organized for the television cameras . . . Milosz seemed convinced that the demonstration had something to do with him. From then on the CKVU interview was one misunderstanding and communication breakdown after another. Milosz was proving to be a most sensitive and difficult man to work with and television is not known for its responsiveness to sensitivity. I earned an incredible dressing down from the great man which was delivered outside to a gathering crowd. "You must never compromise. I have never compromised, not with the Nazis, not with the Soviets."

At John Oliver Secondary School it became obvious that Milosz would not be mingling with the crowd and had no patience for autographs . . . On the whole his reading style was formal and stiff, his delivery humourless. It was clear from his manner and his prefatory remarks that he takes himself very seriously indeed . . . I personally gained a curious impression of the man whose poetry I had been studying for so long. Aside from not getting along with him and finding him difficult and temperamental, I was left with a widened outlook. It is the quality of being from a vanished world, a country which has disappeared from the map, a culture which is all but absorbed into the Soviet monolith, and a poetic style that is more at home in the nineteenth century than in the twentieth that makes his work unique and important.[164]

Expenses were high for the large event.

Next up was Edward Albee. With the project close to his heart, Tom Ilves invested plenty of energy and labour into this festival that would showcase plays, readings, films and workshops from the quintessentially modern American playwright. The city welcomed the Storefront's efforts in bringing this theatrical giant to Vancouver. Local writers and students of dramatic arts were promised a unique opportunity to work with Albee in the context of a workshop. Anyone thinking of a flutter and enrolling for the sessions was reminded that the fee was tax deductible, and that few things look finer on a resume than studies with one of the major playwrights of the twentieth century.

Accordingly, the Storefront would stand in as the rehearsal site of Albee's play *The Zoo Story*, directed by Roy Surette of Carousel Theatre. Albee would make himself available to comment and answer a few questions about his work. Compounding the glee among theatre and stage folk was another Albee play, *Seascape*, to be featured during his stay. Directed by Bonnie Worthington, director of Green Thumb Theatre School, this production would be mounted at Robson Square Media Centre Theatre in the heart of downtown, June 22 to 24. The Storefront was back in the limelight.

Edward Albee

Ilves reviewed the week-long festival (June 21 to 25) in the American playwright's honour.

Following hard on the heels of the Milosz reading, the Literary Storefront mounted an even larger extravaganza, the Edward Albee Festival: a week of plays, films, receptions, workshops, readings—and behind the scenes, a week of frantic postering, printing, stapling, as well as arranging interviews, catering, selling tickets, ushering . . . exhausting but ultimately rewarding.

Fortunately for us, Mr. Albee turned out to be one of the most personable and enchanting visitors we've had at the Storefront . . . [he] tried his utmost to help us smooth out problems, arrange for publicity, even suggesting we offer a special reduced rate for his reading so that people who couldn't afford the benefit price could still attend. But what struck us as most important and refreshing was Mr. Albee's keen interest in young artists and unconventional and experimental attempts at developing the arts, including efforts like our own Literary Storefront.

This attitude was most apparent in the workshops . . . Albee's twenty-five years of prominence have in no way dulled his receptivity or interest in new work. He read the submissions in the Creative Writing seminar with the care one misses in far more "intensive workshops" and was so impressed with the efforts of several participants that he made a special effort to call them back, give additional criticism and offer to take the work with him to New York to see about getting it published or produced . . . What better way to provide for our local talents the recognition they deserve than to bring the powers here?

Similarly, in the acting and directing workshops, Mr. Albee not only talked refreshingly about the craft of directing, but he moreover provided the participants with some keen insights about how a playwright conceives his work to appear on stage. This proved especially illuminating in the discussions of the two plays performed as a part of the Albee Week . . . It became thoroughly clear that Mr. Albee not

only writes engaging and moving plays, but that regardless of genre, he is one of the outstanding writers of our time.[165]

As Ilves told the *Vancouver Sun* during an interview, "Well-known people like Spender and Albee do come in to Vancouver, but then they speak only at UBC or SFU. That makes them inaccessible to people who aren't students. The rest of us folks don't know what's happening.[166]

The numbers on these events are evidence of the seriousness of importing such international figures: ticket sales for the Albee and Milosz events netted $5,434, with the Albee workshops another $2,460. Albee's daily retainer was $1,500, while the cost of bringing Milosz was, again, U.S. $2,802.10.[167] The Polish Community had chipped in $50. A veteran like Spender ran $975. From a local poet's or artist's perspective where a month's rent still ranged from $300 to $450, the costs for Storefront headliner events were becoming seriously steep.

Whether they could be sustained at this calibre was anyone's guess.

The minutes of the board of directors meeting of July 9, 1982, shed light on the Storefront's financial situation. Hildi Adelhelm, Wayne Holder's wife, presented a financial statement and passed around copies. It noted that $6,000 would be coming from the BC Cultural Fund and that an accounts payable balance of $3,500 existed for the ambitious Edward Albee Festival from June. Noteworthy is the mention that Alouette Search Services, Ltd., a real estate title search company was owned by Adelhelm and Holder, loaned the Literary Storefront approximately $12,500. It also donated a $500 to the Storefront. The Vancouver Poetry Festival Society, of which the couple were directors, donated an additional $400.

In practical terms, in the early 1980s, that loan from Holder and Adelhelm's company to the Storefront equalled the down payment on a reasonable house in a good area of Vancouver; it was a serious commitment. At the following August board meeting, directors agreed that this debt to Holder and Adelhelm would be repaid in monthly sums of between $100 and $250.[160]

At the same meeting, a motion was forwarded by Ilves and passed by the board to strike a "non-voting Advisory Board" for the Literary Storefront. A considerable number of prominent names from the Vancouver arts community were proposed. Such a board would perhaps have brought added respect to requests for organizational and funding support; however, action on this initiative does not appear to have flourished in further business.

According to Bill Jeffries, from the artists' collective upstairs:

No sooner had Tom and Wayne landed than they wanted to make bigger things happen. They wanted not to have a local place; it was part of their plan to make something big happen . . . spending money on the likes of Edward Albee. It was an interesting example of kind of misjudging the world, thinking that other people shared your interest.[161]

At the local level, some things remained the same, particularly the scuffling that's part of every writer's life. Illustrating what local poets were doing to survive, the September newsletter brought the following note from poet and publisher bill bissett in his idiosyncratic diction:

bill bissett announces representative colleksuynuv his current art paintings on display at the literaree storefront.

he advises that the price on them is ½ (50%) off the alreadeereasonabel prices: all payment terms considered: evreething must go to help save blewointmentpress at the bank.

Another cue card turned up in October when the newsletter was renamed the *Literary Storefront Monthly*. Emphasis would be on the literary-critical dimension, and Ilves and Holder were listed on the masthead as the editorial board. Holder was leading an Author's Night that month on William Everson, also known as Dominican Brother Antoninus. Everson, a revered figure in North America's fine press printing community was also the founder of Archetype West, an imprint series dedicated to a critical formulation of regionalism in writing from the American West. Holder's inquiry would measure the aesthetic demands of the artist's response to landscape rather than Modernism as a foundation for the development of a distinctive regional poetic.

Holder and Ilves would also bring Everson to Vancouver for an intimate evening reading at Robson Square. Victoria poet and publisher Richard Olafson still considers that event one of the most memorable in his long career:

I was living in Banff and came out all the way for Everson. When he read he was bent and shaking with Parkinson's and the fringes on his old buckskin jacket were just vibrating, shaking all over. He was like a mystical presence, a shard of pure energy, it was in his eyes. He gave an entrancing reading; the audience wasn't that large, it was sprinkled in a big room, and I don't ever remember another to compare with it. It's stayed with me: even though they're writers, some of these guys are elevated beings. They have something else; a few have that charge. I spoke to Everson afterword and he repeated my name; "Scandinavian . . . I'm Norwegian," he said. I was thrown back when he shook my hand, I couldn't handle it, the pure energy in his eyes. He had the fire.[168]

A follow-up note of thanks from Everson to the Storefront organizers in a style reminiscent of Issa read, "A fragile dewdrop on its perilous way from a tree's summit. Good show."

Not all the Storefront's volunteer base and supporters were fully on board with the changes that Ilves and Holder had in mind, although many others were impressed with their ideas and energy. Among a number of the old guard, there was unease regarding the new artistic direction. At the root of Storefront supporter dissatisfaction was, as Fertig states:

> most likely that they were from the U.S. and they had a very ambitious focus that was in ways disconnected from the collective/ community spirit of what and why the Storefront had begun, and core funding really needed stabilizing before shooting for the stars. Slow growth would have been more sustainable. It was a Canadian literary centre and the grassroots membership was the bedrock.[169]

In a 1983 letter to Robert Bringhurst, Ilves indicates his lofty creative aim. He was hopeful of turning Vancouver "into the cultural capital of the Western Hemisphere."[170]

When this difference in managing style fused with aspirations to do bigger things and increase public visibility of the Storefront further, critics began to knock that style. As Fertig states, a critical element for remaining board members was the Storefront's always-precarious funding. With the Storefront just beginning to find its feet regarding provincial arts support, the organization's own constitutional mandate was coming into conflict with administrative practice. Former board member Claudia Cornwall, says:

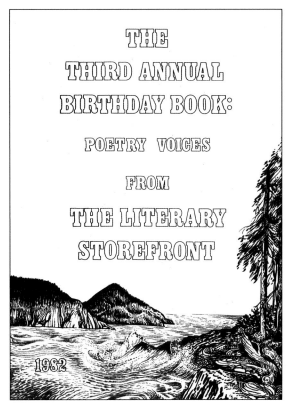

THE
THIRD ANNUAL
BIRTHDAY BOOK:
POETRY VOICES
FROM
THE LITERARY
STOREFRONT

1982

I think because they were kind of grandiose, bringing all the names, that some people dropped away from the L.S. as a result. I don't think they were able to attract a new group of people. They brought in some, but not enough.[171]

Yet whatever bumps transpired, there was always time for fun. Cat Majors and bill bissett—"yes th brillyant literaree storfront!"—who had a new book of poems for children, paired up for a Halloween Children's Masquerade at the end of the month. Bissett was still esteemed for being identified by Jack Kerouac in his view, back in 1968, as the best young poet in North America. There was also a *Third Annual Birthday Book* in 1982. Printed in a limited edition of 500 copies by Orca Sound Publications, it was designed by Cathy Ford and Dona Sturmanis and had various editors in celebrating the third and fourth years of the Literary Storefront.[xiv]

On October 27, 1982, Tom and Wayne put in the Literary Storefront's third BC Cultural Fund application. The purpose of the grant was for "operating assistance to continue the level of activity of the past year . . . and to expand the Literary Storefront monthly to a full-

---

xiv   Contributors were Winona Baker, Peter Baltensperger, Marilyn Boyle, Jan E. Conn, Jane Court, Gayle Fisher, Hosea Hirata, Laura Jones, R.A. Kawalilak, Penny Kemp, Sarah Kennedy, D. Long, Tim Lander, Seymour Mayne, Francesca Newton-Moss, John Patrick, Joe Poet, R.J. Rankin, David Satherley, Al Todd, Lorraine Vernon, ElJean Wilson, Carolyn Zonailo, with cover by Tora.

fledged journal of reviews, for typesetting, and for three part-time salaries for a Director, and Editor / manager for the Monthly, and a volunteer co-ordinator / office manager.[172]

They requested $40,000, an enormous increase from the $6,000 received earlier that year. Expenses projected were $69,500, which included $19,200 for posters and newsletters (design, production, printing). Total revenue expected was $69,500, with ticket sales at $14,000 and membership at $3,500. Their plans for development and new activities stated:

We have decided not to keep our space . . . [as] the rent of $450 a month has become prohibitive to us . . . [we want] to find a space which is at street level and more visible to the public, a true "store-front" . . . the largest readings would be held at alternative spaces such as libraries, schools or the Robson Square Media Centre . . . we have been discussing the possibility of cooperating with other groups to try to get a low rent for writers organizations through the city of Vancouver . . . resumption of publication [newsletter] . . . publishing an expanded events calendar . . . telephone campaigns to build up membership and recruit volunteers . . . corporate sponsorship of the Distinguished Writers Series . . . gala benefit readings . . . a renewed emphasis on workshops and classes.[173]

It was an ambitious ask of a provincial government that maintained a Scrooge-like supervision of the public purse during a period of deep economic recession in Canada. They waited for the outcome.

On November 19, Mona Fertig returned to read at the centre she'd founded four years previous. In a postcard to the board of directors on November 23, she must have been pleased that the Storefront had survived because she wrote, "It is good to see that the Dream has not died! I wish you all the best in re-creating the image of the Storefront. Especially as a group with a sense of COMMUNITY. Best of luck." In a week of headliner name appearances, she was followed in town on November 25 by Alberta fiction writer W.P. "Bill" Kinsella—then one

George Faludy, Robin Skelton,
Classical Joint, Photograph
by Trevor Carolan

of Canada's hottest properties with his novel *Shoeless Joe*, which would become the smash film *Field of Dreams*—and by Michael Ondaatje, twice winner of the Governor General's Award for Poetry.

While her own reading was greeted with collegial warmth, Fertig wrote later that she had learned from members of increasing alienation among Storefront supporters from the new Ilves-Holder style of leadership. "And there were issues concerning exclusiveness . . ."[174] "The committees I'd worked so hard to establish began to dissolve," she noted.[175] Despite palpable unease within the larger Storefront clan, after her restful eight months away, Fertig was very reluctant "to step into the situation."

At his reading, Kinsella had a taste of the state of things too. A year and a half earlier, he had been accorded a warm welcome at the Storefront:

There was a crowd of over sixty very enthusiastic listeners and I sold a lot of books . . . what I remember is that at the end of the evening an enthusiastic fan left me a joint on the table where I was signing books. I said, they shouldn't, but they insisted. Since neither my wife nor I ever drank or used drugs, I left the joint on the shelf of the podium as surprise for someone.

The second appearance was Nov. 25, 1982. I flew into Vancouver and no one met me. I believe that was my first but not last experience of being ignored by organizers who booked appearances for me. I took a taxi to L.S. and met Wayne Holder . . . The disorganized organizers had made no arrangements for accommodation, so I went to see Bill Hoffer and he agreed to house me. There was a crowd of about 70 and I only sold 15 books.[176]

It had been another year of first-quality, if unevenly organized,

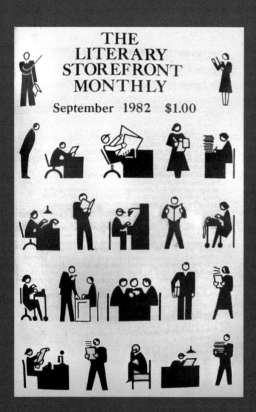

THE
LITERARY
STOREFRONT
MONTHLY
September 1982 $1.00

THE
LITERARY
STOREFRONT
MONTHLY

GEORGE FALUDY
WED., NOV. 10th

NOVEMBER, 1982
ONE DOLLAR

LITERARY
STOREFRONT
MONTHLY
December 1982 $1

Elizabeth Smart Reading!!!

reading performances, and it was not over yet. Sam Hamill, the Cascadian poet and translator, made a visit from Port Townsend, Washington, and George Faludy arrived again in November when he read at the Classical Joint. After him came one of the more interesting poets of the day, Antler, on December 8—a pre-eminent voice in the American work-poetry scene, and published by City Lights. To the astonishment of many in Vancouver's literary scene who frankly were not aware that she was still living, novelist Elizabeth Smart dropped in from her redoubt on the Sunshine Coast to read—an event known as the Distinguished Writers Series—that was as exotic in its rarity as it was genuine community homage to a true literary master. The reading was scheduled a block from Robson Square. For devotees of her classic novel *By Grand Central Station I Sat Down and Wept,* which recounts the heartbreak of her long love affair with English poet George Barker, and her most recent book of poetry *A Bonus,* with its brilliant title-poem celebration of artistic perseverance, Smart's reading was not simply an occasion, but a form of literary grace. Renee Rodin remembers, "One [reading] highlight was tough-talking, chain-smoking, sneaker-clad and totally vulnerable Elizabeth Smart. I could hardly believe we were in the same room breathing the same air."[177]

Yet the event was not unblemished. Poet-novelist Theresa Kishkan had a sense that the Storefront's old collegial ambiance was already diminishing:

I recall a reading at the oyster bar in the Manhattan apartment building on Thurlow, I think it was, and how Elizabeth Smart was shepherded in, given a pompous introduction, and how the atmosphere was very, very unpleasant. She gave a good reading, but her handlers were awfully nervous that she might actually mingle with audience members afterwards and removed her from a conversation I was having with her."[178]

Standing: Karl Sturmanis, Robert Tyhurst, Tony Seldon, Unknown. Sitting: D.M. Fraser

9

1983: And Now for Something Completely Different

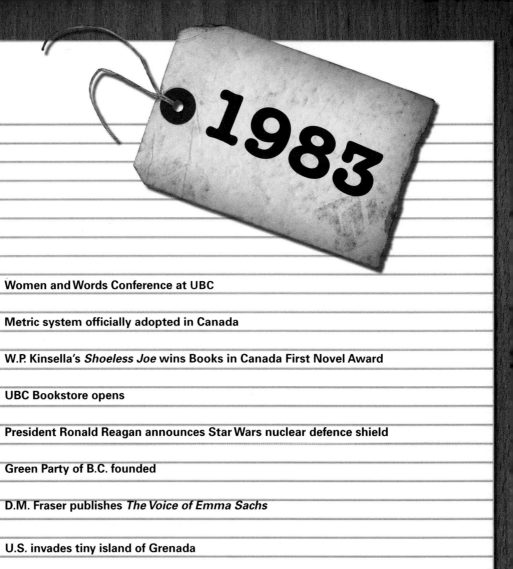

1983

Women and Words Conference at UBC

Metric system officially adopted in Canada

W.P. Kinsella's *Shoeless Joe* wins Books in Canada First Novel Award

UBC Bookstore opens

President Ronald Reagan announces Star Wars nuclear defence shield

Green Party of B.C. founded

D.M. Fraser publishes *The Voice of Emma Sachs*

U.S. invades tiny island of Grenada

BC Place opens

The Sechelt Festival of the Written Arts established

Michael Jackson introduces the "moonwalk"

Stan Rogers dies in an Air Canada flight

The first newsletter of the year arrived with a radically different appearance. In a front-page note that announced "Another New Beginning," editor Tom Ilves explained how, as the descendent of the Literary Storefront newsletter, the new journal, titled the *Vancouver Literary News* (VLN), would now serve as the Storefront's official organ, while effectively functioning as a literary magazine.[179] Wayne Holder and John Gould are listed as editorial assistants; Hildi Adelhelm and Merry Bullock, the wives of Holder and Ilves respectively, are noted as being responsible for production. Acknowledgment is made for the continuing funding support of the government of British Columbia through the BC Cultural Fund.

A back-page addition reported

The Vancouver Literary News is the direct descendant and continuation of the *Literary Storefront Monthly*. From here onward it will also function as a magazine of reviews and features. If you had a subscription to the *Monthly*, you have a subscription to the *News*. If you didn't, don't you need one?

The contents were significantly different and included strong articles by Peter Eliot Weiss and Nigel Hunt on the state of theatre in Vancouver. *Talking Dirty*, a frothy, gossipy hit stage show by local playwright Sherman Snukel, had entered its second year, Weiss wrote; and Anne Mortifee, one of Vancouver's most enduring popular singers, had just enjoyed an unexpected winter seasonal hit with her musical *Reflections on Crooked Walking*. Meanwhile, the elfish, money-spinning director Larry Lillo was directing a new play, *Garage* by David King. A further theatre/literary arts note came in an obituary for Tennessee Williams, who'd had two openings of his plays in Vancouver in the past three years and had developed affection for the city.

Christine Burridge filed a report on the first Vancouver Antiquarian Book Fair that was held at Robson Square Media Centre, a venue that the Storefront realized could prove useful for larger literary events. Toronto rare-bookseller David Mason brought special copies

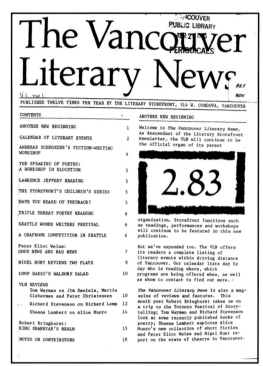

The Vancouver Literary News

PUBLISHED TWELVE TIMES PER YEAR BY THE LITERARY STOREFRONT, 314 W. CORDOVA, VANCOUVER

Vl no l

2.83

ANOTHER NEW BEGINNING

Welcome to *The Vancouver Literary News*. As descendant of the Literary Storefront Newsletter, the VLN will continue to be the official organ of its parent organization. Storefront functions such as readings, performances and workshops will continue to be featured in this new publication.

But we've expanded too. The VLN offers its readers a complete listing of literary events within driving distance of Vancouver. Our calendar lists day by day who is reading where, which programs are being offered when, as well as whom to contact to find out more.

The Vancouver Literary News is also a magazine of reviews and features. This month poet Robert Bringhurst takes us on a trip to the Toronto Festival of Storytelling; Tom Wayman and Richard Stevenson look at some recently published books of poetry; Sheena Lambert explores Alice Munro's new collection of short fiction and Peter Eliot Weiss and Nigel Hunt report on the state of theatre in Vancouver.

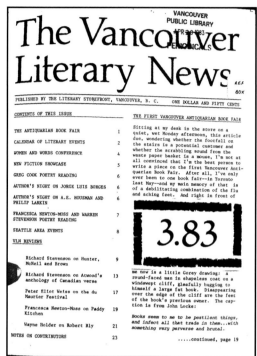

The Vancouver Literary News

PUBLISHED BY THE LITERARY STOREFRONT, VANCOUVER, B. C.   ONE DOLLAR AND FIFTY CENTS

3.83

THE FIRST VANCOUVER ANTIQUARIAN BOOK FAIR

Sitting at my desk in the store on a quiet, wet Monday afternoon, this article due, wondering whether the football on the stairs is a potential customer and whether the scrabbling sound from the waste paper basket is a mouse, I'm not at all convinced that I'm the best person to write a piece on the first Vancouver Antiquarian Book Fair. After all, I've only ever been to one book fair--in Toronto last May--and my main memory of that is of a debilitating combination of the flu and aching feet. And right in front of me now is a little Gorey drawing: a round-faced man in shapeless coat on a windswept cliff, gleefully hugging to himself a large fat book. Disappearing over the edge of the cliff are the feet of the book's previous owner. The caption is from John Locke:

Books seem to me to be pestilent things, and infect all that trade in them...with something very perverse and brutal.

.....continued, page 19

of *Tennessee Williams in Tangier* for the Fair, translated and signed by the esoteric Paul Bowles, who translated Mohamed Choukri's original. The event marked Vancouver's first exposure to a real market for author-signed books, broadsides and fine press editions, and attendance was strong. In a more literary shade, Tom Wayman and Richard Stevenson reviewed recent poetry titles, and Sheena Lambert assessed Alice Munro's latest collection of short fiction. The VLN, it was announced, would appear in twelve editions per year.

The calendar of literary events continued to report on forthcoming readings and projects. Simon Fraser University professor Peter Buitenhuis was leading a book discussion group at the downtown Grosvenor Hotel; Andreas Schroeder had a six-week fiction-writing workshop ahead; Toronto playwright Lawrence Jeffery would read, followed a week later by Judith Roche from Seattle and the Bumbershoot Arts Festival, along with the former and current editors of *Prism International*, St. John Simmons and Richard Stevenson. In a broadening exercise, Francesca Newton-Moss was offering a Storefront newbie titled The Speaking of Poetry: A Workshop in Elocution. Colin Browne was gearing up to teach a workshop on interviewing, and Robert Bly would read out at UBC.

The strongest material came in Robert Bringhurst's report on the Toronto Storytelling Festival. "King Shahryar's Realm" elevated the level of reportage substantially and marked a period of involvement in Literary Storefront activities by the poet.

In the early 1980s, Vancouver theatre achieved what will likely be regarded in the future as its golden age. Peter Elliot Weiss's newsletter report[180]on the New Play Centre's 9th Annual Du Maurier Festival demonstrated how the quality of Vancouver's playwriting community had meshed seamlessly with its organizational and business chops. A scan of his information regarding the playwrights and their works is illustrative of what Vancouver's theatre scene was producing, and its quality, at the time: Tom Cone (*Herringbone, Cubistique*); John Lazarus (*Dreaming and Duelling, Midas*, and soon his hilarious *The Late Bloomer*); Sheldon Rosen (*Ned and Jack, Frugal Repast*); Tom Walmsley (*White Boys, Something Red*); Sherman Snukel (*Talking Dirty*); Christian Bruyère (*Walls*); Leonard Angel (*The Unveiling*); Campbell Smith (*Timestep*); Richard Ouzounian (*British Properties*); Betty Lambert (*Clouds of Glory*); Ted Galay (*After Baba's Funeral*); Margaret Hollingsworth (*Operators*); Tom Grainger (*The Great Grunbaum*); and, of course, George Ryga's *The Ecstasy of Rita Joe*, which had put a tiger in the tank of local playwriting. It was a formidable array.

On April 8, 1983, a letter from Tom Fielding announced that the grant awarded to the Literary Storefront from the BC Cultural Fund would only be $7,500. It advised, "Since the grant approved was less than the amount requested, we will require a revised and balanced budget, reflecting any necessary changes in expenditures and programs. This must be returned before May 15."[181] "Insufficiently clear reporting" was stated as why the grant was not more, and they were asked to do a cash flow and revised budget, and appeal info was enclosed with a sample cash flow sheet. Ilves replied to Fielding on April 21, appealing the grant decision, stating emphatically:

The reasons [for our appeal] are based on information obtained since October 1982 . . . and are as outlined below

Underestimation of the costs of the *Vancouver Literary News*. Critically and popularly successful as it might be, the reincarnated Storefront publication costs more than anticipated . . .

A. . . .In the application we stated we were printing the magazine ourselves. The results, to our dismay, were not worth the savings: few people, either writers or readers considered a magazine as poorly printed as the old *Literary Storefront Monthly* worth reading, buying or subscribing to. With the quality work produced by a professional printer--and offered to us at considerably reduced rates--we have upgraded the appearance to a point where we sell out our issues at bookstores, attract new readers and the attention and writing of some of the province's leading writers . . .. the printing bill has increased too. Our latest issue, 800 copies at 40 pages each, cost us $751.

B. Mailing costs . . . have become outrageous . . .

C. Contributor's fees: . . .we have to offer some remuneration . . . prominent writers have been forthcoming and eager to help us out.

The grant application did not perhaps make sufficiently clear the need for meeting the administrative costs . . . nor . . . how much time the operation of the Storefront and the VLN would take... Finally it may not have been clear to the Cultural Services Branch how substantially the Storefront has changed since its last grant application... nor perhaps . . . how much these changes were due to the efforts of the two principal administrators...

. . .Clearly, we've evolved into a major cultural organization . . . these changes have come about through the efforts of administrators with considerable experience in business, management, and editing. There is a cost to a set of programmes as extensive and successful as the Storefront's... the time and efforts of the administrators . . . have been donated up til now . . . To accomplish these goals, Holder and Ilves have had to work full-time. That kind of commitment cannot be sustained for long; there is a long and venerable tradition to the failure of arts organizations: in which support lags too far behind growth, those responsible get fed up and leave, the organization loses much of what it has gained. The Storefront has already gone through one such cycle; it would be a pity to repeat it and see one of the provinces unique institutions revert to its erstwhile muddling, amateur status.

We ask therefore that the Cultural Fund reconsider and provide some funding for administrative salaries . . . Detailed financial information for the purposes of the appeal will be forthcoming.[182]

Around the town, an unusually full slate of events was scheduled, adding to whatever the Storefront had planned. Czech novelist Josef Skvorecky, living in exile in Toronto, was giving lectures on film and culture at SFU, Duthie Books, and talks for the Readers' Book Club series at the Grosvenor Hotel. B.C.'s champion of social justice issues, the playwright/novelist/screenwriter George Ryga was appearing at the West End Community Centre; Aritha van Herk and Patrick Lane were reading on separate dates at Kwantlen College and the downtown public library; and Frank Davey, Nicole Brossard, Robin Skelton, playwright Sharon Pollock, Jack Hodgins, Ralph Gustafson, Kevin Roberts, Sandy Frances Duncan, Brian Fawcett and Raymond Hull were all reading in the Vancouver and Victoria areas.[xv]

At UBC Robert Bringhurst, who had led a writers' workshop the

---

xv   Spring readings at the Storefront included Trish Hopkinson, Randolph Maxted, Marion Quedneau, Lidia Alexandra Wolanskyj, Greg Cook from Nova Scotia and an afternoon meet-and-greet book-signing with Phyllis Webb, Jane Munro, Rosalind McPhee and Carole Itter.

previous summer that by popular demand was offered again in the spring, was heading a seminar called The Process of a Book with guests Elizabeth Cleaver, Jan Truss, Suzanne Martel and Bertrand Gauthier. Bringhurst's involvement with typography and fine press traditions would result some years later with his acclaimed publication of *The Elements of Typographic Style* that would be translated into ten languages. In the April edition of the VLN, Wayne Holder would offer his analysis of Bringhurst's recently published poetry collection *The Beauty of the Weapons*. The polymath Bringhurst would also contribute a report on a Children's Literature Roundtable at UBC for the VLN.

Advertising made a greater appearance in the newsletter too. The Coburg Gallery, located across the hall from the Storefront, promoted its photographic exhibitions by Lorraine Gilbert and Shane Coursault.

Notices for William Hoffer's Granville Street bookstore also began to appear. Cumulatively, efforts toward the newsletter's production were holding steady. The versatile production group numbered Hildi

Adelhelm, Merry Bullock, Erik Nordholm and Dona Sturmanis.[xvi] In July they would be joined by a young editorial assistant from the Dallas Peterson group, Douglas Coupland. He would also place a classified advertisement with two telephone numbers soliciting work: "Designer seeks lay-up work, both traditional and modern. Contact Douglas Coupland Jr. who is both a traditional and modern person. Rates negotiable per project."

Within the deeper structure of the Storefront's identity, which had drawn original and early Storefront members into a cohesive community, had been a core commitment to writers and writing from the beginnings, from the fermentative stages—a kind of passionate localism. In its inherited cross-cultural traditions from B.C.'s Pacific Coast ethos was a view that it was okay to work, write and publish from the periphery of a larger, eastern-dominated literary world. The region's particular cultural and environmental knowledge now situated Vancouver at the centre of the emerging culture of the Pacific Rim, and writers and poets here were at the heart of new world "multiculture" beat that was beginning to throb internationally and unstoppably. Unconsciously, through its grassroots ethos that welcomed and encouraged new voices and new ways of expressing the word and language, the Literary Storefront had been serving as a stepping stone in the evolution of multiculturalism within the arts and literary community.

The nature and scope of the Literary Storefront's original view was shifting in shape. For Ilves, Holder and the newer group that was helping to guide plans and make decisions, it wasn't so much that hometown was ho-hum, as that "downtown" could also be big time. The shift in emphasis from the Storefront's earlier grassroots orientation was increasingly evident.

---

xvi   Newsletter volunteers included Ellie Claiborne, Richard Clements, Claudia Cornwall, John Gould, Trish Hopkinson, Brett Matthews, Randy Maxted, Geoff Mitchell, Francesca Newton-Moss, John Patrick, Richard Stevenson, Karl Sturmanis and ElJean Wilson.

The Literary Storefront, drawing by Joe Rosenblatt. From the Blackfish Press Reading broadside (Jim Green, Albert Moritz, Joe Rosenblatt, Allan Safarik). A signed limited edition of 100.

Three months following her return to the West Coast, Fertig wrote to the board on February 13, 1983, in defense of the Storefront's membership, its constitution and its original spirit: "My recent re-involvement is only as an Advisory Board member and believer in its egalitarian dream which is difficult in this egotistical age, but something that makes this place all the more valuable and worth working for," she wrote. "I created this place to break down walls, not to build them." Later that month, in a final break, she and Peter Haase would remove the last of their personal belongings from the Cordova Street centre. Gone went the Sylvia Beach doll, the large photographs of Shakespeare and Company, the signed guest book, the framed pictures of writers who had read during Fertig's time, the large round workshop table Peter had built.[183] The den-mother was gone. And so was Dallas Peterson Associates.

For Dona Sturmanis, it was getting hard to feel the love in the room. "Towards the end it was a bad scene which is why we left," she recalls in an email. "Tom and Wayne wanted me out because I did not agree with what [they] were doing. I did see Wayne on the street one time and he apologized, saying he was making amends."[184]

In April, Michael Bullock of UBC's Creative Writing department joined the newsletter production team, another in the growing link of associations with academic culture. The Storefront was becoming a logical next step for some after studying (or teaching) creative writing at the august Point Grey campus.

Importantly, the newsletter was publicizing an upcoming bilingual conference at UBC:

From June 30 to July 3, women from across Canada will gather [in] Vancouver 1983 for the Women and Words Conference at UBC. The scope of the conference is wide: it will include women with all levels of experience and specialties that relate to all aspects of the written word: writers, editors, printers, booksellers, academics, teachers, critics, librarians, and publishers. The conference seeks to provide the context for an exchange among women from diverse cultural backgrounds including Native and Quebecois, to name only two.

The Storefront joined in the call for volunteers and billets for participants. Themes during the three-day conference were Women and Words: Tradition and Context, Doing It! Power and Alternative Structures, and New Directions.

Coordinated by poet activist Betsy Warland, the conference had been her idea, and she pulled together a committee and then went for funding. Warland became the paid co-ordinator with Victoria Free-man.[185] The bilingual conference was a resounding success and drew almost one thousand women from writing, publishing and scholarly backgrounds. It proved to be a genuinely revolutionary gathering and subsequently led to years of communication among women writers in Canada. Unapologetic that it was a women-only event, conference organizers allowed space for a wide horizon of topics that included race, ethnicity, systemic disenfranchisement of women from deci-sion-making structures and similar hot-button issues. Of keen interest

National Book
Festival poster

to Western Canada women was the opportunity to engage in dialogue with their francophone counterparts from Quebec, New Brunswick and smaller communities that included Métis women.

Helping set the agenda on the opening night at UBC's Old Auditorium, Louise Cotnoir from Quebec proclaimed: "Words are illusions; words distort; language is biased and (women) are the ones who suffer this bias. We are the sub-basement of language . . . We are fighting against the social order that has defined us by its language."

When male reporters from Vancouver's daily newspapers complained about the event's gender-exclusive nature, women journalists took over the task. UBC's student newspaper *Ubyssey* reported a typical female writer's situation: in a workshop session addressing economic issues and how they impact women's writing, Helen Potrebenko pointed out her experiences as a female working-class novelist and poet. "I learned about literature through the rejection letters I got from publishers," she relates. Before her gritty novel *Taxi!* was published, Potrebenko had received thirty rejections.

When the allocation of Canada Council grants was brought up, the prevailing situation of male-dominated juries was revealed: in the previous ten years, only 28 per cent of all grants to individual writers had gone to women. The situation in academe was not much different: a mere 12.5 per cent of Canada's tenured academics were women.[186]

April additionally brought Shakespeare's 419th birthday and a toothsome National Book Festival week to Vancouver. In a public event, Robin Blaser moderated a three-hour panel discussion at Robson Square Media Centre addressing the topic of Western Canada as a Literary Region with Rosalind MacPhee, Brian Brett and Charles "Red" Lillard. In another Storefront-sponsored event at the same downtown uber-nexus, an indication that Storefront readings were moving to satellite locations, Constance Rooke (*Malahat Review*), Fred Candelaria (*West Coast Review*), Richard Stevenson (*Prism International*), Leona Gom (*Event*) and Sharon Thesen (*Capilano Review*) considered the question, What part does an editor play in magazine publishing?

Lunchtime readings at Robson Square featured industry-centred poems by Kirsten Emmott, Phil Hall, Zoe Londale, Tom Wayman, David Conn, Mark Warrior and Calvin Wharton. And for children, Cat Majors presented Lulu the Clown's Birthday Party, a poetry reading for children of all ages. As well, Christie Harris doubled up with illustrator Doug Tait for a children's fiction and slide show presentation titled *Where Do Monsters Come From?*

The now regular participation by playwrights took the form of a powerhouse line-up reading their works-in-progress: Sherman Snukal, Leonard Angel, John Lazarus, Peter Weiss, Mary Schendlinger, Glenda Leznoff, David King, Steve Petch, Marc Diamond and Peggy Thompson.

The third edition of the VLN shows that its "editorial office" was now at 3167 West 6th Avenue in Kitsilano, Ilves' home neighbourhood. With the improved layout and design, the newsletter now sold for $1.50. By the double issue #5-6 (May-June), advertisements from publishers were appearing: Pulp Press, Talonbooks, Peregrine Books and MacLeod's Books. Doubleday had a full-page promoting Paul St. Pierre's novel *Smith and other Events.* The back cover noted a forthcoming reading appearance by poet-translator W.S. Merwin, under the auspices of the Storefront at the Robson Square Media Centre—its fourth major reading under the direction of Ilves and Holder.

The open readings and feedback sessions that were a Storefront staple now occurred more frequently, with poetry and prose sessions alternating weekly. Kids and big kids alike could look forward with relish to nightly readings for three weeks on CBC Radio's *Booktime* of Kenneth Grahame's children's classic *The Wind in the Willows.* And The Writers' Union quietly reported that its new contact was B.C. Rep Jan Drabek, novelist and future Czech ambassador.

Poetry in the newsletter came from Brian Brett, Rosalind MacPhee and J. Michael Yates. Audrey Thomas sent in a lovely story entitled "A

Pair of Queens," recounting the simultaneous appearance in town of Her Majesty Queen Elizabeth on her latest Royal Tour and bon temps roulette Zydeco accordioniste Queen Ida. Robin Ridington kept up critical standards with an offbeat essay on "Shamanism and Laurie Anderson." The Storefront flag was flying, as ever, just a little to the left.[xvii]

After an afternoon reading by Audrey Thomas and Leon Rooke, I once headed out for coffee in pelting rain with Tom Ilves and Richard Stevenson, the editor of *Prism International*. We ended up in a little Hungarian place and ordered goulash. Ilves was delighted and said he thought that he was back in New Jersey or somewhere, and that he hadn't seen a little place like this since leaving the Apple.

The Storefront would be closed for July and August, but not before Intermedia veteran Ed Varney—poet, publisher, Dadaist—would don his mortarboard to instruct a seminar on poetic license. It promised an opportunity to "come to class and see if you've learned your stuff."

Editor Ilves signed off in the newsletter before the break with a Fertig-esque appeal for renewed volunteer initiatives:

There are volunteer positions open for every skill and every level of commitment . . . We need painting, carpentry, clerical help, receptionist and phone answering work, and assistance in crewing special events and readings. Bartenders and visual artists, letter-writers and clean-up volunteers, all are needed . . . You've got a good business head? Join the fundraising committee. If you like what's going on, come in and help. If you don't like what's happening, come and straighten us out.

The appeal for a significant increase in the BC Cultural $7,500 grant was not successful. At the year-end annual general meeting, October

---

xvii   Late spring/early summer readings at the Storefront would bring Atlantic Canada's prolific Silver Donald Cameron, Sharon Doubiago of Port Townsend, Bill Bradd of Montreal and Norm Sibum; Celtic performance poet-singer Isabelle Baillie; Surjeet Kalsey; Ron Kawalilak; Crispin Elsted; Beverley Simons and a Writer's Group event with Anne Marriott; ElJean Wilson; Lidia Wolanskyj; Jane Munro; Leon Rooke and Audrey Thomas; and Elizabeth Gourlay. The Second Annual International Sound Poetry Festival had Americans Lorris Essary, Karl Kemptom and Dan Raphael trucking in.

23, 1983, ElJean Wilson recalls there was concern from the board that the Storefront was in debt a fair amount of the time, and complaints were raised again about what some felt was a lack of inclusion in Storefront decision-making. Part of the debt would be forgiven; however, Claudia and Gordon Cornwall who served on the board were uneasy, for example, about the level of possible financial liability involved in promoting what they felt were overly ambitious events like the Albee Festival. "The numerous big names . . . the numbers were starting to be scary," Claudia Cornwall reflects:

I didn't want to be on the Board where there might be a $10,000 liability . . . I went along with it for a while, but it cost a lot of money to fly these people out, put them up in a hotel. It wasn't like they were already doing a book tour of western Canada. The Literary Storefront had to bear most of the cost. It was nutty . . . Also, I was less interested in what they were doing. It wasn't Canadian, local . . . It had been more exciting when I didn't care about who the people were or not. I just wanted to go and listen to what was new, get an impression, make up my mind and be changed or not.[187]

At the AGM, accounts payable showed $3,869 owed, including rent from August to November of $1,785. The Westin Bayshore Hotel was owed $398 and the Printing House, $759. There was a general discussion of the current situation and future. Minutes of the meeting report:

Chronic shortages of cash and volunteer energy remain major problems, rendered critical by the announced intention of Wayne Holder and Tom Ilves to withdraw after a year and a half of very generous commitment of time and energy. Wayne informed on the financial situation of the organization: Unforgiven debts were estimated at $2,000 - $3,000.[188] Various proposals were discussed, including shutting down . . . the rent of $450 a month, no longer shared by sublessees, was too great . . . New members of the Board were elected—Sharon Barber, Robert Bringhurst, Trish Hopkinson, Francesca Newton-Moss, Robert Stelmach, Richard Stevenson, ElJean Wilson.

It was moved that the Centre's premises be vacated by the end of the month. The motion carried.[189]

On the back of the minutes is written:

Other members made generous offers of their time and resources, and, like a phoenix, the Storefront rose once again from its ashes. The current incarnation is so young that we can't yet see what shape it will take. That will depend on what people put into it. But although fetal, it is certainly alive.[190]

On December 15, 1983, treasurer, ElJean Wilson and board member, Frances Newton-Moss submitted the fourth Literary Storefront application to the BC Cultural Fund. It requested $14,000:

for operating assistance to renew and expand services and activities in the community . . . to secure new premises for a more accessible street level drop-in information and events centre. Our goal is to revitalize the Literary Storefront following its recent decline in activities which resulted from the unexpected resignation in the fall of both the VLN editor [Tom] and the managing director [Wayne] due to personal commitments. The members of the Board of Directors are prepared to do everything possible to continue the vision of the founder [Mona] and the effort of many volunteers over the past five years of the Literary Storefront's history.[191]

It was a big drop from the previous year's request, and they had to state why the original budget was not realized. Five ways of saving expenses were listed:

1. Eliminate hotel accommodation for outside readers.
2. Drastically reduce printing costs by not resuming the VLN and by having all materials typewritten only.
3. Reduce special events budget rentals.
4. Reduce rental expense.
5. Reduce salary to co-ordinator.[192]

It was a hopeful attempt to rally once again. The Storefront was preparing for another year on the stormy seas of literature.

Sylvia Beach in Gastown
'Read Canadian Poetry' by Ed Varney

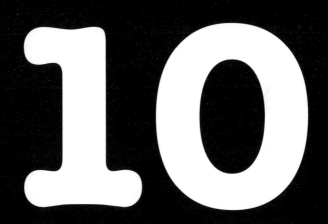

10

1984–1985:
The Late Innings

1984-1985

Bhopal plant chemical catastrophe in India

Canadian mortgage rate "falls" to 13%

Prime Minister Indira Gandhi assassinated in New Delhi

Pierre Trudeau announces his retirement

Josef Skvorecky wins Governor General's Award for Fiction with *The Engineer of Human Souls*

Bookseller Bill Duthie dies

Bryan Adams wins four Juno awards

Vancouver Downtown Eastside Residents Association establish DERA

Audrey Thomas is first winner of the Ethel Wilson Fiction Prize for *Intertidal Life*, now awarded annually

Horrific famine in Ethiopia intensifies

The Space Shuttle Discovery takes off on its maiden voyage

Official opening of the Granville Island Brewery, first Canadian microbrewery

Wayne Holder and Tom Ilves ran the Storefront's operations for eighteen months. The marquee writers they brought to the city enhanced its already established reputation as a literary centre. The Storefront was still seeing new faces in the crowd too, but these were ironically often of a different character than the grassroots elements that had originally kept the centre moving along. The university literature students, theatre fans and teachers who were drawn to the higher-calibre events were less likely to have the time to dedicate themselves as volunteers with a literary community in Gastown. As veteran committee volunteers wearied and drifted away or took up new challenges, they were not replaced. Some were members who were alienated by what they felt was a more urbane, autocratic direction. The Storefront's committee structure began to dissipate.

By late 1983, the Storefront was slightly in debt, with expenses of $18,186 over revenues of $17,647; $13,300 was from grants alone.[193] More critically, organizational energy had evaporated—"People retained hope, but they didn't have the energy to keep carrying on" according to ElJean Wilson. Tom Ilves had written grant applications that noted how importantly support was needed for an administrative salary to continue building the Storefront's operations, but like Fertig's persistent efforts before him, the results were less than encouraging. Holder and Ilves would leave Vancouver permanently by the early spring of 1984, a period when they travelled to Estonia, then a part of the Soviet Union. Nevertheless, the remaining troops rallied, and there was a new board. Facing a limited future, in a drastic existential move, the board quit the Cordova Street premises at the end of November, as had been decided at the AGM, and the phone was disconnected. Gordon Cornwall and the board moved the Storefront materials to ElJean Wilson's basement in West Vancouver.[194]

Winding down a creative arts centre is seldom an edifying experience. Bill Jeffries got the Storefront's fifty black wooden chairs for his gallery, then passed them on to the Kootenay School of Writing

(KSW), founded in 1984 following the B.C. government's closure of David Thompson University Centre in Nelson. This new writers' centre that had relocated to Vancouver on Broadway at Oak brought an energy and sense of determination with it that in some ways echoed the Storefront's own early educational mandate. The Kootenay School would also eventually receive a generous share of the Storefront's library,[195] absorbing it into what would become the Charles Watts Memorial Library, named in honour of the late special collections librarian from Simon Fraser University.

Synchronicities between the fading arc of the Storefront and the growth and work of the KSW after 1984 are worthy of additional study. It has been observed that a number of the writers associated with the Kootenay School—Tom Wayman, Fred Wah, Daphne Marlatt and others—had all read at the Storefront.[196]

Nineteen eighty-four proved a defining year. Without a centre to radiate from, and with a decline in memberships, the Storefront endeavored to survive. Despite the many obstacles, the newsletter was now essentially a calendar of events, and it continued to be produced by Robert Stelmach and ElJean Wilson out of her husband's business office.

"In spite of these changes, we have not thrown in the towel," Stelmach, the newsletter editor wrote, reassuring readers that "the recent AGM led to the appointment of a new Board of Directors committed to reviving and revitalizing the Storefront." He worked to revitalize the newsletter, upping the ante and turning it into "an arts magazine covering all the arts in the Lower Mainland."

Almost synchronistically, as the Storefront was declining, the Federation of BC Writers also began organizing more readings and workshops, or was approached to do this by publishers and some of its supporter, professional literary organizations. Modest support funding from the Province that might otherwise have gone to the Literary Storefront enabled the Federation to keep readings going, mainly in the immediate Gastown area. The Federation readings and workshops borrowed in spirit straight from the established Storefront model and took place in the Classical Joint coffee house, local restaurants and occasionally pubs near the old Storefront premises. Later, when post-Expo 86 real estate pressures began affecting downtown properties, Federation readings moved for some years to the La Quena restaurant on Commercial Drive in Little Italy, again following the Literary Storefront model of multiple readers, a conversational community focus, interplay between readers and the audience, and often as not, concerns with social justice.

George Orwell's fateful 1984 was not without activity or vision at the Literary Storefront. Though reduced in nature and scope, events continued to be offered using Duthie Books and assorted community art spaces; board meetings also continued. In the 1984 treasurer's annual report, ElJean Wilson reported revenues of $4,550, including a grant of $2,000 from the City of Vancouver, over expenses of $4,492. The Storefront was still breathing, but its pulse had weakened.

The April board meeting recorded news of a John Newlove reading in the spring and a reimbursement of his expenses of $100. The Storefront also paid for Phyllis Webb's hotel bill. In June the barometer took a fatal drop when the minutes reported that that the BC Cultural grant was not applied for, partly due to lack of preparation time and because the Storefront now lacked a space. Reapplying for the grant was contingent on that core factor.

Still, there were ideas. Robert Bringhurst suggested hosting a monthly literary soiree open to all Storefront members and volunteers in order to strengthen the feelings of community and commitment. It was an appeal straight from Mona Fertig's original playbook. ElJean informed the board that they now had only forty-five members. Even so, the board learned that discussions were under way with K.O. Kanne and Alice Niwinski from the City of Vancouver about acquiring a share of a common literary arts space.

Programming notes showed Tom Cone reading at the Coburg Gallery, and two Storefront-sponsored workshops were confirmed: Joan Haggerty would lead Finding Your Voice on September 22, and Richard Stevenson would offer Tapping the Literary Market on October 11. Both would be held at the Community Arts Council boardroom. Francesca Newton-Moss would renew feedback sessions in the fall.

In retrospect, it was too much to take on. Within a few months, Robert Stelmach realized that "the skills and time to save the Literary Storefront's magazine" were beyond his capacity. In a letter to the author, he observed, "By cancelling the newsletter, it was clear, I was also marking the demise of the Literary Storefront. It was one of the hardest decisions I have ever made."[197]

Hindsight might have kept the newsletter simple, or perhaps continued trying to organize readings and workshops. But the collective drive was no longer there.

Several Storefront members did attend a meeting on October 5 held at the Canadian Book Information Centre, titled Writers Un-Ltd. In attendance were Alice Niwinski of Social Planning (City of Vancouver), Gloria Greenfield of Women and Words, Glen Downie of Vancouver Industrial Writers Union, K.O. Kanne (writer-at-large), Carolyn Zonailo of the Federation of BC Writers, Robert Stelmach of the Literary Storefront and Lidia Wolanskyji of the Literary Storefront.[xviii] K.O. Kanne recorded the minutes and wrote:

The original purpose of the meeting was to gather [as] many writing groups as possible together to discuss the idea of a permanent space within the city for writers . . . This has been an idea fermenting

---

xviii Absent from the meeting were ElJean Wilson, the Literary Storefront; Alan Safarik, League of Canadian Poets; Betsy Warland, Women and Words; Sherman Snukel, Playwrights of Canada; Audrey Thomas, Writers' Union of Canada; Colin Browne, Kootenay School of Writing; Christopher Moore, ACTRA; Bev Olandt, PWAC; Tony Gregson, Association of BC Book Publishers.

in the minds of a number of groups. The model to begin with is 24 Ryerson Ave. in Toronto. The environment seems ripe for the fruition of this idea in Vancouver. There is an urgent need for affordable reading, meeting, and office space. It may only be limited by our imaginations, so allow yourself to dream a little.[198]

At time of writing, thirty-one years later, this same idea is still being discussed with the City and the Province with a steering committee of the ABPBC and supporters.[199]

By January 1985, even the last of the old brigade were exhausted. With few members attending the AGM, a vote was taken to dissolve the Friends of the Literary Storefront Society. A final letter from ElJean Wilson said, "The Storefront played an important role in the development of Vancouver's literary community, and we had hoped to keep it alive . . . Here's to all the people who have worked for the Storefront over the years and to the writers and readers of British Columbia."[200]

In a 1985 letter to Wilson, Robert Stelmach, one of the last board members, notes that he had been in communication with Jeff Derksen of the Kootenay School of Writing concerning a possible "happy home" for the Literary Storefront's library. Regarding the collection of tape-recorded readings at the Storefront over the years, Paris Simons of CITR Radio at UBC had confirmed that the student-run station was to either copy or store these tapes. Peter Grant of Vancouver Co-operative Radio (CFRO) (and later CBC), however, suggested that his station and the main branch of the Vancouver Public Library join forces to collate and archive the project. Together, they could apply for funds for blank tapes, studio time and an archivist. Fortunately, the library ended up acquiring the tapes. ElJean Wilson took the Storefront archives to UBC and struggled for months to organize the Storefront's finances and final reports.

As Shakespeare writes, the rest is silence.

Water Street, 1974, Vancouver Archives CVA 1135-44,
Photograph by William Eadington Graham

11

Dispersion: What Remains

"...there's already an air of defeat to these stores
angled modishly together like lobster traps
mixed with a courtful of rain and
the computer-like roar of a steel band..."

from "Remembering My Youth at the Opening of Gaslight Square"
—Eldon Grier letter to Mona Fertig, 1978

Alan Twigg has noted how, in retrospect, the Literary Storefront was "one square in an enormous quilt."[201] If Vancouver's literary arts scene has flourished in recent decades though, no small thanks is due to the pioneer work of Mona Fertig and the Storefront—which according to Ann Cowan, founder of Simon Fraser University's Writing and Publishing Program, greatly inspired SFU's work. "Cowan says she was encouraged by the community of interest and enthusiastic following for writers in Vancouver exemplified by the storefront."[202] Since the heyday of the Literary Storefront, British Columbia has witnessed a constant flowering of the literary arts. These days, as Robert Stelmach has noted, other organizations have taken up some of the grassroots work once performed by the Literary Storefront, such as Pandora's Collective and the now common community writers' groups and clubs, including the long-running Burnaby Writers' Society, Royal City Arts Society and others in White Rock and South Surrey. In Vancouver, the annual fall Vancouver Writers Festival founded by Alma Lee in 1988, who was succeeded in 2006 by Hal Wake, thrives as a literary bonanza of readings, seminar discussions and special events. No listing of important successors would be complete without noting the fourteen-year-long series of readings that took place regularly at R2B2 Books (formerly Octopus Books, whose reading series was run by Brownie and her partner Jules Comeault) on 4th Avenue, run by Renee Rodin and Billy Little, and subsequent owners. Many writers associated with the Storefront were welcomed there. In the early

1990s, Michael Turner of Hard Rock Miners band renown coordinated a reading series at the Malcolm Lowry Room in the Admiral Hotel on Hastings in North Burnaby.

Perhaps unsurprisingly, in an interview with *Poetry Canada Review* in 1980/81, Fertig articulated her idea of what the Literary Storefront might evolve toward, or encourage:

> My dream for the Literary Storefront was that it would grow and become a communication center for writers—that they would exchange ideas and it would become very stimulating; that we would transcend all the personal and political games and at some point could all come together and have one of those international festivals.[203]

Then presciently she observed, "That may be a few years away though."[204]

Alma Lee, former executive director of The Writers' Union when Mona was running the Literary Storefront, eventually moved to Vancouver and related to Fertig years later in the 1990s that the Literary Storefront had been a source of inspiration in starting the Vancouver Writers Fest.[205] Meanwhile regional writers' festivals continue in Salmon Arm, Victoria, Whistler, the Sunshine Coast, Kootenays, Mission and numerous Gulf Islands. City book prizes are awarded annually in Vancouver and Victoria; both have also formally instituted poet laureates, as have New Westminster and Nanaimo. SFU's Writing and Publishing program under the direction of coordinators like Betsy Warland and Wayde Compton has thrived. Keeping track of it all and maintaining a crucial public focus on B.C. writers and book publishing has been *BC BookWorld*, established by Alan Twigg in 1987, that thrives as Canada's "largest-circulation, independent publication about books." It is distributed free on BC Ferries and in librairies, community centres, educational institutions and bookstores throughout British Columbia.

If the prevailing social climate for books and literature has shifted, Vancouver's arts and cultural scene *in toto* has undergone a seismic shift since the mid-'80s. There's scarcely a week on the calendar without a cultural, ethnic or arts discipline-specific festival taking place at one venue or another—dance, film, music, comedy, theatre, spoken word and sub-genres of every description.

Yet looking back, before the wholesale internationalization of this Pacific city, the Literary Storefront could still represent something locally original that was unique.

Dona Sturmanis sums up the ordinary magic:

What I remember is the fellowship . . . Maxine Gadd preparing her next poetry manuscript there or now-bestselling novelist Douglas Coupland deciding to become a writer rather than an artist, as he was then. There has been no place like it since, nor will there ever be, for its spontaneous cultural centrifugal force.[206]

Years later, like many others, Jan Westdendorp still feels the old Storefront vibes:

The rooms of 314 West Cordova grew much quieter after Mona left and the Literary Storefront closed. These days, I occasionally have reason to go back there because a client for my book design and typesetting services, Whitecap Books, is nestled between the Literary Storefront's old back rooms and the stairwell leading to the third floor TBA-TV used to occupy. Every time I go back there, I hear and feel again the halls echo with the voices Mona brought to ring in that building.[207]

After the Storefront

After Mona moved back from Montreal and Peter from Australia, they returned to their house on Joyce Road. Mona worked part-time at Classic Books, a block from the Literary Storefront, as well as at Ariel Books on 4th Avenue, Vancouver's only women's bookstore. She served as West Coast columnist for Poetry Canada for two years, and in 1983, they bought a Beach Grove cottage in Tsawwassen, where they were married in the backyard. Mona's artist father died two months later. In 1984, the year the Literary Storefront closed, their daughter Sophia was born, and Mona began work on *A Labour of Love*, an anthology of poetry on pregnancy and childbirth that took four years to complete. "It kept me connected with my literary roots," she says. "It kept me centered. I was living away from what was happening in Vancouver, from my writer friends, and it was often a lonely time, me and babe, especially with Peter working out in North Vancouver."

Fertig helped found the BC Book Prizes and worked to name the Poetry Prize after Dorothy Livesay. As a member of the League of Canadian Poets during the late 1980s, she helped organize the Honouring our Foremothers reading at the National Library in Ottawa. In 1988 their son Paris was born, and they lived in the historic community of Ladner for three years. At this time, she returned to the literary fray as BC/Yukon Rep of PEN during John Ralston Saul's presidency. This regional group worked for the release of Vietnamese Buddhist monks and prisoners of conscience Thich Tue Sy (who was eventually released) and Thich Tri Sieu, imprisoned for their writing. Members of this chapter were Daniel Francis, Jane Covernton, Ernest Hekkanen, Michael Hetherington, Keath Fraser, John O'Brian, Jay Hamburger, Robin Mathews and Trevor Carolan.

While attending the International PEN Congress in Toronto and Montreal in 1989, Fertig was inspired by the emerging writers and languages she heard from around the world. Subsequently, for four years, she published (m)Öthêr Tøñgués, a small international literary periodical.[xix] After her family moved to Salt Spring Island in 1990, Mona

---

xix Contributors included Siphiwe Ka Ngwenya, Adriana Batista, Stacy Creamer, Erin Moure, Thich Tue Sy, bill bissett, Roma Potiki, Kim Morrissey, Yuki Hartman, Tsvetanka Sofronieva, Elizabeth Allen, Dorothy Livesay, Joyce Parkes and Duo Duo. Plus Marguerite Pinney, Ann Diamond, Willie Ka Tshaka, Mark Sutherland, Jane Covernton, Sharon Negri, Ronnie R. Brown, Kim Chi-Ha, Li Min Hua, Memoye Abijah Ogu, Deena Padayachee, Hans Raimund, Loreina Santos Silva, Fritzi Harmsen Van Beek, Nam Hunt, Tanya Lester, Ioannidou-Stavrou, Antonio D'Alfonso, Artuo Arias, John Barlow, Dorin Tudoran, Sandi Johnson, Muriel Karr,

and Peter began publishing collector-quality limited edition chapbooks of Canadian poetry and letterpressed broadsides.[208]

On Salt Spring, Peter added letterpress printing to his repertoire under the tutelage of legendary master printer and typographer Jim Rimmer of Pie Tree Press, as well as other letterpress printers on the coast. Under his hand, their labour-intensive publications employed traditional craftwork, letterpress covers and his beautiful original linocuts in signed and numbered editions. Renowned West Coast collector and bookseller Richard Hopkins has since acclaimed the quality of Haase's and Fertig's work.

For over ten years, Fertig worked part-time at Volume Two Books, and she and Peter opened a writer's retreat on their property. From their island base, the pair continue in Literary Storefront fashion to organize writing, book art, letterpress printing workshops, book launches, exhibitions and readings. Fertig also served as The Writers' Union BC/Yukon Rep, 2001-2003, and is a founding member of Writers West and Canadian Writers Against Google (CWAG), and of Salt Spring Writers and Friends, which offers writing prizes to graduating Gulf Island Secondary School students.

In 2008 Fertig used the funds received from selling her Literary Storefront archives to the University of British Columbia, along with a grant to write a book on her father, to found Mother Tongue Publishing, a British Columbia literary trade publishing company. Mother Tongue's focal point is The Unheralded Artists of BC, the unprecedented series of illustrated biographies. The Great BC Novel Contest that it additionally pioneered has been a hit-maker from the beginning when inaugural winner Gurjinder Basran's *Everything Was Good-bye* received multiple awards and citations.[xx] In 2012, Simon Fraser

---

Rhonda Wauhkonen, Mercedes Roffe, Anne Burke, Sigitas Geda, Tim Lander, Liliane Welch, Marie Luise Kashnitz, Tom Savage, D.C. Reid, Marosa Di Giorio, Mark Warrior, Han Shan, Zoe Landale, Eugenio Montale, Richard Trumball.

xx   To date, Mother Tongue has published 27 books www.mothertonguepublishing.com

University acquired the (m)Öthêr Tøñgué Press fonds.

Throughout the years, Mona continues to write poetry. Several of her books were released with various publishers, including *Sex, Death & Travel, Invoking the Moon-Selected Poems (1975-1989)*, *This is Paradise* and *The Unsettled*. Reviewers note that her poetry holds, 'a sensuousness, honour, and a spiritual density,"[209] and that "Fertig writes a devotion to human connections that, like the gardens and seas throughout, root, drown and, amazingly, liberate."[210]

After his Vancouver years, including a short teaching period at SFU, Tom Ilves left to live in Munich, Germany, where he worked for Radio Free Europe, "first as a researcher and foreign policy analyst then later as Head of the Estonia desk in the Estonian section."[211] Following the fall of the Soviet regime in February 1989, he settled in Estonia, adopted the Estonian spelling of his name as Toomas Hendrik Ilves and held a number of organizational positions. He served as Estonian ambassador to the U.S., Canada and Mexico and, like more than a few writers before and since, entered politics. Since 2006 he has been the elected President of Estonia. Living in a small country situated in what he has called "a bad neighbourhood" next to Russia, Ilves has succeeded in guiding his nation forward economically and culturally. The list of honours and decorations he has since received from nations worldwide is exemplary. In recent times, he has had to respond to Russian leader Vladimir Putin's aggressive agenda. Ilves has not been shy, however, in acknowledging his early arts administrative experience in Vancouver. Of his time at the Literary Storefront, his online presidential biography notes, if somewhat inexactly, that he was "Director and Administrator of Art, Vancouver Arts Center, Canada, 1981-1983."[213]

Wayne Holder subsequently returned to the U.S. and published *A Booklover's Guide to the Mission*, which received the 1997 Mission Merchants Association Award for Excellence. Illustrated by Elizabeth Newman, it contains information on the cultural renaissance of the city's South of Market Street area. His papers, including extensive photographs and accounts of life in Estonia during its liberation struggles, are held by the Hoover Institute at Stanford University. Among the holdings is a printout of an article from 2007 by Mona Fertig on the Literary Storefront from the *BC BookWorld* website.[214]

Other key Storefront members dispersed and continued writing, organizing or publishing; some retired, others moved on or passed on. Among the Literary Storefront's heroic worker bees that held the fort at different times for Mona, Tom and Wayne, Dona Sturmanis remains active as a Kelowna journalist, poet, fiction writer, book editor and founder of the city's first writing school. From 1998 to 2002, she ran a cultural salon in West Kelowna, Melvyn's Living Room, inspired by the Literary Storefront. She has taught creative writing for more than 30 years. Robert Stelmach, aka Max Tell, continues to write stories, songs and poetry. In 2014 he was honoured with Writer International Network's Distinguished Author and Artist Award. His songs have been shortlisted in regional and international competitions. ElJean Wilson still houses a few remaining books from the Storefront in her basement. Craig Spence, at time of writing, is the executive director of the Federation of British Columbia Writers. Other stories, untold or forgotten, have mostly disappeared like long-ago travellers, into the mystic, into Gastown's steadily gentrifying streets.

What was it all about? Before the well-meaning but limited-in-experience administrators and data-miners carry on with the project of forgetting and building toward the arts community of the future, like the Zen bard Basho's "temple bell that keeps ringing from the flowers," a brief from the founder of the Literary Storefront may prove timely, especially for the young and aspiring.

Mona Fertig concludes:

The Literary Storefront was amazing as a psychological/sociological dream considering how young I was. It was ahead of its time, yet a product of its time. I welcomed all writers and their work even if their writing didn't interest me, because it wasn't about me. It was about the collective. Growing a wellspring for the literary arts.

My upbringing as an artist's daughter and the unusual depth of my parents' lives deeply influenced me. My dad's exclusionary experiences with art politics was key as well as my parents' discussions and interest in art, politics and Carl Jung. I always wanted, in my own way, to quietly bust open the doors of elitism, level the playing field, inspire a quiet revolution. I remember when I had to write the Storefront constitution for its non-profit status that I consulted George Whiten, who was a director of the Alexander Neighbourhood House, and I told him that I was worried about a board taking over and changing direction and making it less open. He said there wouldn't be much I could do except try to instill the values in the constitution if I could. That's more or less how things finally played out.

In the end, like ripples in the pond, people found jobs through the Literary Storefront, created works, wrote books, found friendship and inspiration, published poems; some found lovers or partners; others became publishers or playwrights, founded groups like the Federation of BC Writers; some began careers and families, some found place; and some even found themselves.

Alice Niwinski, K.O. Kanne, Alan Twigg, Trevor Carolan, Jan Drabek, Federation of BC Writers' event; Malcolm Lowry Brown Bag Mystery Literary Tour, Sylvia Hotel, 1986. Photograph by unknown

Sylvia Beach and James Joyce, from *Shakespeare and Company*
by Sylvia Beach, published in 1956

12

Inspiring and Historic Models

The Poetry Bookshop, London, 1912

The Poetry Bookshop was operated by the poet Harold Monro in London's intellectual Bloomsbury district (1912-1935). It held regular readings and workshops in addition to selling books of poetry exclusively. Monro established *The Poetry Review*, which became influential, partly through his links with Ezra Pound and the rise of the imagism movement. He also used his private income to publish new collections of poetry, though only rarely were they profitable. His premises became an important community node for London's writers: T.S. Eliot's Criterion Club met there regularly during the '20s, and Eliot and Monro were firm friends. At various times, poets including Wilfred Owen and the sculptor Jacob Epstein lodged in rooms above the bookshop. Monro became a deeply respected and popular lecturer in Britain and Ireland.[215]

La Maison des Amis des Livres, Paris, 1915

Adrienne Monnier's La Maison des Amis des Livres bookshop opened on the Left Bank's 7 rue de l'Odéon in 1915. A pioneering woman in the otherwise conventional French business world, she was devoted to literature and sustained friendships with literary personalities such as André Gide and Paul Valéry. Monnier developed her bookshop as a centre for intellectual exchange in the heart of Paris's ancient core. Associated with the modernist impulse, she launched a literary review and began publishing many important French writers of the day. She expressed her own opinions as a critical essayist and collaborated with Sylvia Beach in translating, or introducing writers like T.S. Eliot, Ernest Hemingway and William Carlos Williams to French readership. Following World War II, she continued writing in ill health for almost ten years until taking her own life in 1955.

Shakespeare and Company, Paris, 1919

After World War I, Paris had lost its *belle époque* charm but was still a refuge for international sojourners dodging the moral strictures of home.

Among them was Sylvia Beach, a young American who became an indispensable figure in twentieth-century literary culture. Unlike the triflers who sampled the pleasures of the French capital before heading home with a pocketful of saucy stories, Beach stayed on. Schooled in Paris and Lausanne before the war, she volunteered in the countryside where a shortage of male labour made it more acceptable to wear men's clothes. For seven months, she worked with her sister for the Red Cross in Serbia, helping the wounded in brutal hospital conditions. Her letters reveal how she witnessed the humiliations of women in wartime and in bureaucracies. The experience, she claimed, made "a regular feminist" of her.[216]

After the war, Beach dreamed of running a bookshop. Unsure of the right location, the answer was revealed when she met Montparnasse bookseller Adrienne Monnier. The large, two-spirited Parisienne took the American under her wing, and the pair became lovers. Under Monnier's tutelage, Beach opened Shakespeare and Company, a bookshop and lending library for subscriber-members. The pair ran their respective shops *en anglais* and *en français* across the street from each other, and across the Seine from Nôtre Dame Cathedral.

For North American travellers and expatriates in Europe, Beach's shop became a pilgrimage destination. In addition to lending books, Beach served as a confidante to many writers, as well as providing their *post restante* address. She maintained a supply of quality titles, including the various literary journals, newspapers and manifestoes of the day. The walls she decorated with pictures and signed photographs of leading writers, artists and musicians—D.H. Lawrence, Aaron Copland, Malcolm Cowley and George Gershwin, among others—along with a small original William Blake etching she'd purchased in London.

With only a sketchy knowledge of what she was getting herself into, Beach also undertook to produce and underwrite the costs of a new work by the still marginally known Irish novelist James Joyce. The rest is history. Although his *Ulysses* would earn close to a million dollars in the U.S. alone, Beach saw little of it from the self-absorbed Joyce who caddishly declined to cut her a share.

Fearing arrest by the Gestapo in World War II, she closed down her shop, hid her books upstairs in the little apartment she kept and painted over its well-loved Shakespeare and Company sign. She suffered imprisonment for seven months. Liberation came when war correspondent and former customer Ernest Hemingway arrived with a jeep full of American soldiers, anxious to be photographed for posterity. To his credit, in *A Moveable Feast,* the book that details his Paris years, Hemingway would write of Sylvia Beach, "No one I ever knew was nicer to me."[217]

The Gotham Book Mart, New York, 1920

The Gotham Book Mart in New York was founded on West 45th Street in Manhattan by Frances Steloff in 1920, its sole proprietor through many decades. Steloff worked in New York at Loeser's department store selling corsets before showing an aptitude for selling magazines and periodicals. The job gave her training in book buying, a well-paid trade in pre-television America. She saw an opening for a well-managed bookshop that would give her independence as its proprietor and began her business cautiously with a shingle advertising "Wise Men Fish Here." Her wares consisted of used books, small controversial magazines and art and paintings that hung on the walls.

New York's theatre community noticed her inclination toward stocking craft-oriented books from Europe that were in chronically

Photograph by
Chris Silver Smith

short supply. By turning up hard-to-find texts on costumes, stagecraft, set design and acting technique, Steloff drew actors, then a number of celebrity customers. Little literary magazines that frequently gave beginning writers their first opportunity to get published became a staple of Steloff's store, and they gave the Gotham Book Mart a certain cachet. This was a store where you would find the new, the really modern.

Steloff's business became a promotional hub for the city's flourishing book trade; launch parties were common. Poets, scholars and establishment littérateurs were the likeliest personalities to draw a crowd, and over the years, the shop became a city institution. In 1965, W.R. Rogers published an account of Steloff and her store entitled—what else?—Wise Men Fish Here.

Steloff was also willing to publish an author whom she believed in—Patti Smith was first published in a chapbook by Steloff and the Gotham.

City Lights Books, San Francisco, 1953

Founded by Peter Martin and Lawrence Ferlinghetti in 1953, City Lights Books was the first all-paperback bookstore in the United States. Located at 261 Columbus Avenue in the heart of San Francisco's multi-ethnic North Beach district, it has served ever since as a veritable clubhouse for beat generation writers and followers. Ferlinghetti's backroom press, City Lights Books, also helped many major authors break into print, publishing Allen Ginsberg's celebrated *Howl*, as well as Jack Kerouac, Denise Levertov, Charles Bukowski, Gregory Corso, Sam Shepherd and scores of others. For a time, the store allowed writers to pick up mail there, as bookshops had done in Paris when Ferlinghetti attended graduate school at the Sorbonne. Author readings at City Lights continue to attract both the great and the up-and-coming to this day.

The Poetry Project, New York, 1966

The Poetry Project at St. Mark's Church in-the-Bowery was founded in 1966. Readings had taken place regularly in New York's Greenwich Village and the Lower East Side area from the beat generation of the 1950s onward. Situated at 2nd Avenue and 10th Street, within the umbrella of St. Mark's Episcopalian Church with its long history of social outreach in the Bowery, the Poetry Project began as a readings initiative that was shepherded chiefly by poet Paul Blackburn. A small secretariat that included poet Anne Waldman began administration of the project's reading and publications programs. From its earliest readings, the Poetry Project has continued to provide free writing workshops, monthly open readings, lectures, open Monday performance nights and scheduled Wednesday night readings. It published a mimeographed magazine and a monthly newsletter of general information about poetry and publishing that would become a model for the Literary Storefront's publication. Through its more than forty-five-year history, the Poetry Project has served as a major point of contact for the exchange of information in the American poetry scene.[218]

Archival Holdings

UBC Library, Rare Books and Special Collections

The collected papers from the Literary Storefront are held at the University of British Columbia's Special Collections. Contained within twenty-seven fonds, or boxes, the holdings comprise many audio recordings, pictures and a treasure trove of correspondence, grant applications and all the day-to-day ephemera of running the operation, including financial records, subject files and related printed material pertaining to workshops, readings, fundraising and publishing. Most files relate to general administration, funding, publications and author subject files that include unpublished manuscripts. These include: 141 audio cassettes, 71 photographs, 3 audio reels and 1 photograph album. Literary Storefront correspondence and business files from 1982 onward held at UBC are significantly incomplete. Correspondence pertaining to the Spender, Albee, Elizabeth Smart, and other notable events is regrettably absent.

UBC and the Vancouver Public Library

Sound Recordings of: Lidia Alexander, Jennifer Alley, Hope Anderson, Pat Armstrong, Margaret Atwood, Earle Birney, bill bissett, Carolyn Borsman, Marilyn Bowering, Marilyn Boyle, Robert Bringhurst, Colin Browne, Anne Cameron, Matt Cohen, Sally Cole, Jan Conn, Judith Copithorne, Sylvie-Anne Delalune, Melodie Duff, Sandy Frances Duncan, Crispin Elsted, Kirsten Emmott, André Farkas, Lawrence Ferlinghetti, Ferron, Mona Fertig, Rikki and Cathy Ford, Marya Fiamengo, Sylvia Fraser, David Frith, Maxine Gadd, Greg Gatenby, Larry Geiler, Graeme Gibson, Gerry Gilbert, Lakshmi Gill, Chris Glynn, Leona Gom, Reshard Gool, Paul Gotro, Elizabeth Gourlay, Jim Green, Eldon Grier, Al Grierson, Genni Gunn, Thom Gunn, Britt Hagarty, Daniel Halpern, R.D. Hanson, John Harding, Robert Harlow, Christie Harris, Ernest Hekkanen, Jorg Heyman, Gladys Hindmarch, Jack Hodgins, Avron Hoffman, Rosemary Hollingshead, Margaret Hollingsworth, Ted Hughes, Carole Itter, Beth Jankola, K.O. Kanne, R.A. Kawalilak, Penn Kemp, Eileen Kernaghan, Jack Kerouac, W.P. Kinsella, Theresa Kishkan, Joy Kogawa, Betty Lambert, Zoë Landale, Tim Lander, Scott Lawrance, Richard Lemm, Christopher Levenson, Dorothy Livesay, Liz Lochead, Rosalind MacPhee, Mark Madoff, Cat Majors, Jean Mallinson, Daphne Marlatt, Anne Marriott, Sheila McCarthy, Myra McFarlane, Florence McNeil, George McWhirter, Mark Mealing, Irene Mock, Brian Moore, Albert Moritz, Colin Morton, Erin Moure, Jane Munro, Rona Murray, Susan Musgrave, Al Neil, Morgan Nyberg, P.K. Page, Richard Payne, Marguerite Pinney, Sylvia Plath, Peter Porter, Helen Potrebenko, Al Purdy, Naomi Rachel, Kevin Roberts, Jill Rogers, Joe Rosenblatt, Helene Rosenthal, Norbert Ruebsaat, Allan Safarik, Leslie Scalapino, Bill Schermbrucker, Bob Sherrin, Carol Shields, Maggie Shore, Norm Sibum, Karl Siegler, Robin Skelton, Judi Smith, Steve Smith, Charlene Spretnak, Sylvia Spring, Dona Sturmanis, Karl Sturmanis, Anne Szumagalski, Sharon Thesen, Audrey Thomas, Rose-Marie Tremblay, Conni Tricys, Peter Trower, Richard Truhlar, Robert Tyhurst, David UU, Aritha Van Herk, Ed Varney, Lorraine Vernon, Bronwen Wallace, David Watmough, Mark Warrior, Tom Wayman, Phyllis Webb, Ann West, Susie Whiten, ElJean Wilson, Richard Wright, Joanne Yamaguchi, Ann York, Dale Zieroth, Carolyn Zonailo, Zonko

Bibliography

Beach, Sylvia. *Shakespeare and Company*. Orig. 1956; Lincoln: University of Nebraska Press, 1991.

Beach, Sylvia. *The Letters of Sylvia Beach*. Kerri Walsh, Ed. New York: Columbia University Press, 2010.

Bringhurst, Robert. *Ocean Paper Stone*. Vancouver: William Hoffer, 1984.

Carolan, Trevor. "What A Long Strange Trip It's Been . . . " *Word Works*, Summer 2007, pp. 5-20.

Carolan, Trevor, Ed. *Making Waves: Reading B.C. and Pacific Northwest Literature*. Vancouver: Anvil Press, 2010.

Choukri, Mohamed. Paul Bowles, Trans. *Tennessee Williams in Tangier*. Santa Barbara, CA: Cadmus, 1979.

Cornwall, Claudia. "Rescuer of B.C.'s Lost Artists." *The Tyee*, March 16, 2009.

Fertig, Mona. *On The Road for Poetry*. Toronto: Unfinished Monument Press, 1985.

Fertig, Mona. *The Life and Art of George Fertig*. Salt Spring Island, BC: Mother Tongue Publishing, 2010.

Fertig, Mona. *The Literary Storefront: A Brief History*. Chapbook. Salt Spring Island, BC: Mother Tongue Press, 2007. See www.abcbookworld.com/view_essay.php?id=39

Glassco, John. *Memoirs of Montparnasse*. Toronto: Oxford University Press, 1970.

Hemingway, Ernest. *A Moveable Feast*. London: Penguin, 1973.

Jankola, Beth. *Beat*. Vancouver: Poem Factory, 1994.

Leiren-Young, Mark. "Inside Canadian Publishing." *Globe and Mail*, n.d., 1984.

Literary Storefront Newsletter. 1978-1982.

Longstreet, Stephen. *We All Went To Paris*. New York: MacMillan, 1972.

MacSkimming, Roy. *The Perilous Trade: Book Publishing in Canada*, 1946-2006. Toronto: McClelland & Stewart.

McKellar, Keith. *Neon Eulogy*. Victoria: Ekstasis, 2001.

Rogers, W.G. *Wise Men Fish Here: the story of Frances Steloff and the Gotham Book Mart*. New York: Harcourt Brace, 1965.

Spender, Stephen. *The Thirties and After*. New York: Random House, 1978.

Spender, Stephen. *Journals 1939-83*. John Goldsmith, Ed. New York: Random House, 1986, pp. 442-445.

Twigg, Alan. *Vancouver and Its Writers*. Madeira Park: Harbour Publishing, 1986.

Twigg, Alan. *For Openers: Conversations with 24 Canadian Writers*. Madiera Park: Harbor, 1981.

The Unheralded Artists of BC series, Salt Spring Island, BC: Mother Tongue Publishing.

Vancouver Literary Review, Five editions. Vancouver: The Literary Storefront, 1983.

Zonailo, Carolyn. "The Breathable, Blue Surface: Of Poïesis and Place." Carolan, Trevor, Ed., *Making Waves*

Acknowledgements

This book could not have been compiled and told without the help of many hands. Recollecting the assistance and editorial guidance I received brings back many pleasant memories and a deep sense of gratitude. Original source documentation for this book is from the archival depositories in UBC Special Collections, Vancouver Public Library Special Collections, private collections and personal or email interviews. Promotional flyers, newsletters, old photographs, day-to-day business correspondence, financial info and routine mail-in inquiries—these are what survive. Apart from whatever social and critical interpretations of the Storefront's role may still be kicking about, these unmediated artefacts are what tell the story, for the Literary Storefront was a space that existed simply to make things happen. Accordingly, I would like to express my gratitude to Patti Wilson and the librarians at the University of the Fraser Valley (UFV), and those of the Vancouver Public Library, the University of British Columbia, Special Collections; Jacky Lai, Weiyan Yan and Krisztina Laszlo, the West Vancouver Memorial Library and the Hoover Institution Library & Archives, Stanford University. Catharine McPherson, Archival Assistant with the City of Burnaby Archives, was especially helpful. Paul Taylor, Research Librarian at District of North Vancouver Public Library, Parkgate, provided excellent archival assistance–my special thanks.

Many people contributed to the production of this book. For their assistance in the research and writing of it, the author wishes to thank Susie Whiten, Peter Haase, W.P. Kinsella, Jan Westendorp, Bill Jeffries, Ingrid Klassen, Gordon Cornwall, ElJean Wilson, Theresa Kishkan, Joan Haggerty, Cathy Ford, the late Blanche Howard, Judith Copithorne, Dona Sturmanis, Craig Spence, Alan Twigg, Ed Varney, Robert Stelmach, Renee Rodin, Carole Itter, David Watmough, Richard Olafson and the office of President Toomas Ilves, Tallinn, Estonia. Attempts to interview President Toomas Ilves during the writing of this book were repeatedly thwarted by East European political events. Despite extensive search attempts, interview time with Wayne Holder also was not possible. Information in the book about them is original source, or from reputable media reports. A thank-you to all those who sent in their memories for the 2007 chapbook. Special thanks to my research assistants from UFV, Valerie Franklin and Paul Falardeau, and to all those who kindly granted interviews, provided essential perspectives—notably on the early history of the Literary Storefront—and responded to requests for information or recollections.

I am particularly grateful to Mona Fertig and Mother Tongue Publishing for showing the initiative and taking on the risk of producing this publication, and for hospitality during a research visit to her home with Peter Haase on Salt Spring Island. Claudia Cornwall was a careful, concise reader of the book in its late drafts and made many excellent structural suggestions for which I am especially appreciative.

Daphne Marlatt, Katherine Gordon and Dona Sturmanis offered mindful readings of the work, and I wish to express my collegial thanks for their efforts. The Mother Tongue production team were notably attentive and picked up numerous glitches while improving the quality of the text. My thanks for their fine work to book designer Mark Hand and copy editor Judith Brand. And thank-you to Jason Vanderhill for assistance with photographs from the Vancouver Archives

The Office of Research and Graduate Studies at the University of the Fraser Valley generously provided me with scholarly research support during the research and writing of this book, without which it could not have been completed. Merci.

For her forbearance and support during the long maturation of this work, my thanks and love as ever to my wife, Kwangshik. Gratitude is good medicine: to all those I am not able to name who contributed by putting their shoulder to the wheel of its development and completion, *beannacht libh*, many blessings.

Endnotes

1   Total number of those who attended Literary Storefront events during its full tenure of operations was more than 20,000.

2   Fiamengo and Robin Mathews were outspoken in their defence of Canada's cultural sovereignty. Mathews was passionate regarding the number of American professors imported into the English departments at Vancouver's two universities, UBC and SFU. In 1985, he was involved in an acrimonious dispute regarding a teaching position at SFU. Canadian nationalists, including Fiamengo and Milton Acorn, rallied to his defense.

3   www.thecanadianencyclopedia.ca/en/article/small-presses/ Retrieved November 10, 2014.

4   Carolyn Zonailo, in *The Literary Storefront: A Brief History*, Mona Fertig. Salt Spring Island, BC: Mother Tongue Press, 2007, p. 26.

5   Cathy Ford, email to Mona Fertig, January 4, 2015.

6   David Watmough, interview with the author, July 17, 2012.

7   Cathy Ford, email to Mona Fertig, January 4, 2015.

8   Ron Tabak (1953-1984) burst onto Canada's and the international rock music scene as a hard-hitting vocalist with headliner touring act Prism (Juno Award, Group of the Year, 1981). Ronnie died after being hit by a vehicle while riding his bicycle on Christmas Eve, 1985.

9   Video Inn, the public face of the Satellite Video Exchange Society, started in 1973 as a collective. www.virtualmuseum.ca/sgc-cms/histoires_de_chez_nous community_memories/pm_v2.php?id=story_line&lg=English&fl=0&ex=00000854&sl=9975&-pos=1, retrieved January, 29, 2015.

10 Ibid.

11 Ibid.

12 Judith Copithorne, interview with the author, July 13, 2013.

13 *Life and Art of George Fertig*, ch. 7.

14 Ibid.

15 Unless noted otherwise, quotations from Mona Fertig are from lengthy interviews with the author on December 17 and 18, 2012. Further conversations took place during 2013-2014, and in emails and telephone conversations 2013-2015.

16 Ibid.

17 http://www.bethjankola.com/

18 http://www.abcbookworld.com/view_author.php?id=1862

19 Eileen Kernaghan, email to author, May 22, 2015.

20 Ibid.

21 Mona Fertig, personal papers.

22 Ed Varney, email to Mona Fertig, December 5, 2014.

23 Mona Fertig, interview with the author, December 17, 2012.

24 Mona Fertig to the author, October, 26, 2014. An interesting correlation occurred when Mona and Peter started their letterpress printing and publishing business on Salt Spring. Peter was injured and applied to Workmen's Compensation to be retrained as a letterpress printer. A senior WCB staffer visited the Salt Spring studio, and a training program was laid out with Barbarian Press, Blackstone Press, Jim Rimmer's Pie Tree Press and Anderson Press. WCB approved the retraining program.

25 Judith Copithorne interview with the author, 2012 and August 3, 2013.

26 Ibid.

27 David Watmough, interview with the author, July 17, 2012.

28 Blanche Howard to the author, August 2012.

29 Cathy Ford, email to Mona Fertig, January 4, 2015.

30 Mona Fertig to the author, July 17, 2014.

31 Stephen C. Hopkins described Fertig as "a lovely young woman with a graceful, rounded figure and gentle manner. She wears green velvet, many silver bracelets, a few large silver rings, and yellow lacquer on her nails. Her skin is clear and luminous, her mouth sensual and full-lipped, her eyes a clear, arresting blue. She speaks with an innocent tone and I deduce from her remarks that cynicism and sarcasm are alien to her nature." In "Mona Fertig: Vancouver Poet," 1975, English class, VCC, Langara.

32 http://www.ecuad.ca/75years/tuneinturnon/tunealumni.html, retrieved October 2014.

33 http://ccca.concordia.ca/resources/searches/event_detail.html?languagePref=en&vk=8900, October 2014.

34 http://www.dannykostyshin.com/, retrieved October, 2014.

35 Intermedia Press, 1975.

36 Mona Fertig, *The Literary Storefront: A Brief History*, p. 3.

37 At 4 West Pender Street, Vancouver, B.C.

38 The Vancouver Poetry-Co-op had a core of ten poets and a total membership of about forty.

39 Mona's personal files.

40 *The Literary Storefront: A Brief History*, p. 3.

41 Ibid.

42 May 11, 1977 letter from Stephen Osborne to the Canada Council, UBC Library, Rare Books and Special Collections, Literary Storefront Fonds, RBSC-ARC-1331.

43 Surrey Art Gallery received a grant that enabled them to hire Fertig.

44 Lorna Farrell-Ward, email to Mona Fertig, December 11, 2014.

45 C.E. Chapple, February, 1, 1978.

46 Ibid., pp. 3-4.

47 Letter from Mona's personal archives, August 29, 1977, The Fork, Route One, Galiano Island.

48 Peter Haase, interview with the author, December, 16, 2012.

49 http://www.cwill.bc.ca/search/member_detail/128, retrieved October 2014.

50 Barrie Cook, *Province*, April 17, 1978, n.p.

51 UBC Library, Rare Books and Special Collections, Literary Storefront Fonds, RBSC-ARC-1331.

52 Letter to Mona Fertig, May 11, 1978, UBC.

53 In *The Literary Storefront: A Brief History*, p. 5.

54 Geoff Hancock, email to Mona Fertig, September 9, 2007.

55 *Vancouver Sun*, June 2, 1978.

56 Peter Haase, interview with the author, December, 17, 2012.

57 Jeffries would later head the Presentation Galley in North Vancouver and the downtown Simon Fraser University gallery. Bill Jeffries, interview with the author, July 16, 2013.

58 Ibid. Attacks in Parliament on poet bill bissett and his publisher Talonbooks regarding alleged obscenity were made beginning March 1978. Warren Tallman and the Vancouver Poetry Society organized an ambitious series of readings featuring headliner personalities from the U.S. and Canada, as well as several more locally focused "free speech" events in protest. While Blaser was reading an excerpt from *Black Elk Speaks* at a UBC reading that brought a dozen Vancouver poets to the stage, heckling broke out from the audience when a drunken rowdy was not allowed to have his say from the podium. This followed an invitation in a Vancouver Poetry Society newsletter that Tallman made to audience members regarding public discussion, albeit in a more orderly Q & A style. The issue of who controls free speech became a Vancouver brouhaha, and a series of letters to the editor in the *Georgia Straight* kept the pot boiling. Alan Twigg's lengthy letter in the *Georgia Straight* of March 9-15, 1979, provides outstanding critical insightful and judgment of the whole controversy.

59 In *The Literary Storefront: A Brief History*, pp. 26-27.

60 Gordon Cornwall, interview with the author, December 2, 2013.

61 Dona Sturmanis, email to the author, fall 2012.

62 Cathy Ford, email to Mona Fertig, January 4, 2015.

63 Ibid., November 10, 2014.

64 Ibid., January 4, 2015.

65 The series began with Dorothy Livesay, July 28, 1978.

66 Ibid.

67 *The Literary Storefront: A Brief History*, p. 23.

68 The podium was given to Mona Fertig by Beth Jankola. Jankola picked it up on one of her many thrift shop, garage sale "junking" adventures in the '70s. Hundreds of writers have read at it since 1978, and it continues to be used at many Mother Tongue launches and events, three decades later.

69 Tom Wayman, letter to Mona Fertig, April 21, 2015.

70 ElJean Wilson, interview with the author, August 13, 2014.

71 *The Literary Storefront: A Brief History*, p. 6. Also Daphne Marlatt, email to Mona Fertig, February 18, 2015. "Roy also used the name Blue Mule as the imprint for his self-published chapbooks of poems & images. He opened the gallery some time in the

latter half of the '70s. It was when the barbershop on the ground floor folded and he moved into that space. There's a series of Powell St. photographs he took 1978-80 titled Opposite the Blue Mule. It was still going [after 1983] then as a site not only for the display of visual work on its walls but for multi-media performances."

72   See Barrie Cook, *Province,* May 12, 1978.
73   Joan Haggerty, email to Mona Fertig, October, 2006.
74   Bill Deverell, email to Mona Fertig, November 9, 2006. "I will defer to Joan . . ."
75   The Yorkshire-born Skelton was also Chair of the University of Victoria's Creative Writing Department and founder of the *Malahat Review.* Among his accomplishments were the discovery of poet Susan Musgrave and the advancement of Marilyn Bowering. A colourful figure from the otherwise often self-consciously dowdy academic world, his more than 100 published works include 40 books of poetry.
76   Jean Mallinson to Mona Fertig, 2006.
77   Peter Haase, interview with the author, December 17, 2012.
78   April 1979, Literary Storefront newsletter, UBC Library, Rare Books and Special Collections, Literary Storefront Fonds, RB-SC-ARC-1331.
79   Renee Rodin, email to Mona Fertig, January 9, 2007.
80   Jack Hodgins, email to Mona Fertig, 2007.
81   Daphne Marlatt, email to Mona Fertig, November 4, 2014.
82   In *The Literary Storefront: A Brief History*, p. 25.
83   Anna Jean Mallinson, email to Mona Fertig, August 24, 2007.
84   Carole Itter, email to Mona Fertig, November 1, 2006.
85   Purdy contributed an introduction to Trower's *Ragged Horizons* (McClelland & Stewart, 1978). Trower regards this among the signal triumphs of his raucous, colloquial career.
86   Mona Fertig, interview with author February 8, 2015.
87   Sharon Thesen, email to Mona Fertig, October 30, 2014.
88   See *Goddess Remembered*, National Film Board of Canada, 1989.
89   Bill Horne, email to Mona Fertig, February 18, 2015. As he remembers, "I was one of Warren Tallman's students at UBC in the late 1970s, and helped him and others organize a number of fundraising parties in the fall of 1979 in different Vancouver locations, each of which was based on a particular constituency. Theatre people gathered at one house, academics at another, poets somewhere else, etc. All converged later in the evening at a Hall on East Hastings for a dance with Doug and the Slugs. The place was packed. Together with a mailed appeal, the evening raised enough money to pay for a full page ad in the *Vancouver Province* called 'Vox Populi' [The Writing in Our Time: Seven Benefit Readings for West Coast Literary Presses] in support of the Canada Council and Talonbooks, which were under attack at the time."
90   This is the reading series referred to earlier by Bill Jeffries.
91   Advertisement, *Province,* Friday, September 22, 1978.
92   Cathy Ford, letter to Mona Fertig and author, January 4, 2015.
93   UBC Library, Rare Books and Special Collections, Literary Storefront Fonds, RBSC-ARC-1331.
94   Peter Haase, interview with the author, December 17, 2012.
95   Alan Twigg. *Vancouver and Its Writers*, Harbour Publishing, 1986, p. 36.
96   Claudia Cornwall, interview with the author, December 2, 2013.
97   In December 1979 newsletter, UBC Library, Rare Books and Special Collections, Literary Storefront Fonds, RBSC-ARC-1331.
98   Newsletter, November 1979.
99   Ibid.
100   Jan Westendorp, email to Mona Fertig, November 10, 2014. "TBA-TV (Television By Artists) began as a loose group of students, staff, recent graduates and friends of the BFA studio art program at UBC who worked collaboratively on various projects questioning the points of intersection and divergence between art and commercial mass media . . . the TBA-TV members were Karen Dobin, Bill Jeffries, Pax Robertson, Bob Sherrin, Cindy Trotzuk, Arden Williams, Jan (Koot) Westendorp and January Wolodarsky.
101   Bill Jeffries, interview with the author, July 16, 2013.
102   Jan Westendorp to Mona Fertig, November 10, 2014.
103   Mona Fertig, interview by Dona Sturmanis, *Vancouver Magazine,* April 1982.
104   Peter Haase to Mona Fertig, October 28, 2014.

105   Originally published in the *Birthday Book*, 1980, p. 43.
106   The poster was missing the "e" in Earle Birney's first name, and he was not amused. The "e" was added to every poster before the signing.
107   Mona Fertig, phone conversation with Keith Mallard, February 4, 2015.
108   Randall Ware, Ottawa, to Keith Maillard, March 3, 1980; Mona Fertig to Review show supporters, June 11, 1980.
109   Ingrid Klassen continued to host *The Book Show*, her Sunday evening program on Co-op Radio, 102.7 FM. Though not strictly affiliated, the Storefront maintained close relations with The Book Show.
110   Klassen also featured conversations and talks with critics such as then-freelance broadcaster Eleanor Wachtel, who addressed censorship in her recent article "Our Newest Battleground: Pornography" in *Branching Out* magazine. Interview with the author, August 30, 2014.
111   Blanche Howard, email to Mona Fertig, October 11, 2006.
112   Dona Sturmanis started Orca Sound Publishing in 1977 with her former husband, Karl Sturmanis, to publish *The Greenpeace Book*, one of the first books about Greenpeace. It ended up selling 7,500 copies. Several other books were published after this with the Orca Sound imprint, including *The Siberian Chronicles of Henry Schulz*, which sold over 2,000 copies and went into reprint. Email from Sturmanis to Fertig, May 10, 2015.
113   Cathy Ford, email to Mona Fertig, January 2015.
114   Sandy Frances Duncan, letter to Mona Fertig, 2007.
115   Mona Fertig, notes and letters from her Federation of BC Writers file.
116   Federation of BC Writers brochures #1 and #2 from Mona Fertig's files.
117   With Ingrid Klassen and founder Carolyn Zonailo.
118   "Colourful Stories of Williams's Tenure as Writer in Resident Still Abound at UBC," retrieved October 28, 2014, archive.theatre. ubc.ca/glass_menagerie/subject.html
119   Mona Fertig to the author, November 13, 2014.
120   In 1978, April 1 and 2, Fertig and the others went down for the 2nd annual Women's Poetry Festival of San Francisco. The special guests were 20 Canadian poets. Drawings of the festival are in the first Literary Storefront newsletter. They include Naomi Layton, Kay Boyle and Alta.
121   Cathy Ford, email to Mona Fertig, January 4, 2015.
122   *Literary Storefront Newsletter* Jan. 1981.
123   Andreas Schroeder, email to Mona Fertig, 2007.
124   Interview by Dona Sturmanis, *Vancouver Magazine*, April 1982.
125   Tim Lander, email to Mona Fertig, September 2, 2007.
126   From *On the Road for Poetry*, Unfinished Monument Press, 1985.
127   Cathy Ford, email to Mona Fertig and author, January 4, 2015.
128   *On the Road For Poetry*, journal dates April 6-9, 1981
129   Penn Kemp, email to Mona Fertig, November 7, 2014.
130   Ibid.
131   Maxine Gadd, email to Mona Fertig, November 2, 2014.
132   Email, Diana Hayes to Mona Fertig, May 10, 2015.
133   *Literary Storefront Newsletter*, 42, events sheet. Nov. 1981 UBC Library, Rare Books and Special Collections, Literary Storefront Fonds, RBSC-ARC-1331.
134   Ibid #42, Nov. 1981.
135   *Newsletter*, March, 1982."
136   Dona Sturmanis, letter to Mona Fertig, March 1, 1982.
137   Report to Literary Storefront board, UBC Library, Rare Books and Special Collections, Literary Storefront Fonds, RBSC-ARC-1331.
138   Mona Fertig, letter to Tom Fielding, UBC Library, Rare Books and Special Collections, Literary Storefront Fonds, RBSC-ARC-1331.
139   UBC Library, Rare Books and Special Collections, Literary Storefront Fonds, RBSC-ARC-1331.
140   Cat Majors, email to Mona Fertig, 2007.
141   Maxine Gadd, email to Mona Fertig, 2007.
142   Peter Haase, interview with author, December 18, 2012.

143 Mona Fertig, email to author, March 2015.

144 ElJean Wilson, interview with the author, August 13, 2014.

145 Ingrid Klassen, interview with author, August 30, 2014.

146 Mona Fertig to the Literary Storefront board, March 30, 1982.

147 Cathy Ford, email to Mona Fertig, January 4, 2015.

148 Letter from Ingrid Klassen, March 1, 1982, to Mona Fertig and the board of directors of the Literary Storefront.

149 Bill Jeffries, interview with author, July 16, 2013.

150 Douglas Coupland, email to Mona Fertig, November 22, 2006.

151 Newsletter, May 1982, #48.

152 Stephen Spender, *Journals: 1939-1983*, John Goldsmith, Ed., 1986, pp. 442-445.

153 Ibid.

154 *The Literary Storefront: A Brief History*, p. 20.

155 Ibid.

156 At PEN's 54th World Congress in Toronto, 1989, Spender invited a number of writers for a walk along the city's harbourfront, including conference visitors from Vancouver, and discussed publishing conditions at that time compared to when he was a younger writer in London. Typical sales figures for books of poetry remained uncannily static. It was of great surprise to learn that the now-celebrated and heavily anthologized poets of the '30s were often so little read in book form by their own generation.

157 Jennifer Alley, letter to the board, n.d., UBC Library, Rare Books and Special Collections, Literary Storefront Fonds, RB-SC-ARC-1331.

158 Ibid.

159 Ibid.

160 Literary Storefront records are unclear as to whether Holder and Adelhelm received repayment of their loans.

161 Bill Jeffries, interview with the author, July 16, 2013.

162 Ibid.

163 Tom Ilves, letter to Charles-Auguste Lavoie, September 17, 1982, UBC Library, Rare Books and Special Collections, Literary Storefront Fonds, RBSC-ARC-1331.

164 Literary Storefront newsletter, July 1982, UBC Library, Rare Books and Special Collections, Literary Storefront Fonds, RB-SC-ARC-1331.

165 Ibid.

166 Leslie Peterson, "Literary Storefront on the Rise," *Vancouver Sun*, June 21, 1982.

167 Ibid.

168 Richard Olafson, email to author, August 27, 2013.

169 Mona Fertig, interview with the author, Dec. 16, 2012

170 Tom Ilves, letter to Robert Bringhurst, April 12, 1983, UBC Library, Rare Books and Special Collections, Literary Storefront Fonds, RBSC-ARC-1331.

171 Claudia Cornwall, interview with the author, December 2, 2013.

172 Grant application to the BC Cultural Fund, October 28, 1982, UBC Library, Rare Books and Special Collections, Literary Storefront Fonds, RBSC-ARC-1331.

173 T.H. Ilves, grant application to BC Cultural Services Branch, Victoria, October 28, 1982.

174 Mona Fertig, interview with author, March 2015.

175 *The Literary Storefront: A Brief History*, 2007, p. 11.

176 W.P. Kinsella, email to the author, August 22, 2012.

177 Renee Rodin, email to Mona Fertig, January 9, 2007.

178 Theresa Kishkan email to the author, August 2012.

179 In January 1983, Tom Ilves consulted Robert Bringhurst on design of the reformatted newsletter (February 2, 1983, Vol. 1, No. 1) and explained that it would become a main focus. He added, "To prevent this publication from becoming the Vancouver Literary noose I've been working on a Canada Council grant." UBC Library, Rare Books and Special Collections, Literary Storefront Fonds, RBSC-ARC-1331.

180 Literary Storefront Newsletter, February 1983, UBC Library, Rare Books and Special Collections, Literary Storefront Fonds, RBSC-ARC-1331.

181   UBC Library, Rare Books and Special Collections, Literary Storefront Fonds, RBSC-ARC-1331.

182   Letter, T.H. Ilves to Tom Fielding, April 21, 1983. UBC Library, Rare Books and Special Collections, Literary Storefront Fonds, RBSC-ARC-1331.

183   Notes, Mona Fertig to the author, November 13, 2014.

184   Dona Sturmanis, email to Mona Fertig, August 27, 2007.

185   Betsy Warland, email to Mona Fertig, December 16, 2014.

186   See Julie Wheelwright, *Ubyssey*, Summer 1983, Vol. II, No.2, July 1.

187   Claudia Cornwall, interview with the author, December 2, 2013.

188   Literary Storefront financial report, December 7, 1983, UBC Library, Rare Books and Special Collections, Literary Storefront Fonds, RBSC-ARC-1331.

189   Annual General Meeting, the Vancouver Literary Centre, October 23, 1983, UBC Library, Rare Books and Special Collections, Literary Storefront Fonds, RBSC-ARC-1331.

190   Ibid.

191   Box 15, UBC Library, Rare Books and Special Collections, Literary Storefront Fonds, RBSC-ARC-1331.

192   Ibid.

193   Literary Storefront income statement prepared by ElJean Wilson for the period of January 1, 1983–December 31, 1983, UBC Library, Rare Books and Special Collections, Literary Storefront Fonds, RBSC-ARC-1331.

194   Some boxes of books still remained as of October 2014.

195   The gift to the KSW was facilitated by Tom Wayman and Robert Stelmach; Mona Fertig to the author, November 13, 2014.

196   In an interview with Peter Grant, Colin Browne, one of the originators of the KSW, outlines its early period in Vancouver. *Pacific Rim Review of Books*, No. 11, Spring 2009, pp. 7-19, 28.

197   Robert Stelmach, email to the author, September 14, 2014.

198   UBC Library, Rare Books and Special Collections, Literary Storefront Fonds, RBSC-ARC-1331.

199   Association of Book Publishers of BC website, http://books.bc.ca/literary-arts-centre-vancouver/, retrieved May 14, 2015.

200   UBC Library, Rare Books and Special Collections, Literary Storefront Fonds, RBSC-ARC-1331.

201   Alan Twigg, to the author, December 15, 2014.

202   Ann Cowan, email to Mona Fertig, April 14, 2015.

203   Mona Fertig, interview with Robert J. Rankin, *Poetry Canada Review*, Winter, 1980/81.

204   Ibid.

205   Fertig recalls her conversation with Lee in the early 1990s.

206   Dona Sturmanis, email to Mona Fertig, August 25, 2007.

207   Jan Westendorp, email to Mona Fertig, November 10, 2014.

208   There are 28 in the series. They included: Stephanie Bolster, Lorna Crozier, Kate Braid, Cathy Ford, Maxine Gadd, Shirley Graham, Penn Kemp, Robert Kroetsch, Sylvia Legris, Peter Levitt, Daphne Marlatt, Susan McCaslin, P.K. Page, Murray Reiss, Nadine Shelly, Peter Such, Phyllis Webb and Patricia Young.

209   Review in *Prairie Fire* by Andrew Vaisius, Vol 11, No. 3, 2011.

210   Review in *Canadian Literature* by Antje M. Rauwerda, Issue #206, 2011.

211   http://www.britannica.com/biography/Toomas-Hendrik-Ilves, retrieved June 28, 2015.

212   http://www.theguardian.com/world/2011/nov/03/president-ilves-made-estonia, retrieved June 28, 2015.

213   www.president.ee/en/president/biography/index.html, retrieved December 8, 2014.

214   Box 1. Folder 2 contains the History of The Literary Storefront, article 2007. Retrieved February 17, 2015, www.oac.cdlib.org/findaid/ark:/13030/kt02903or6/entire_text/

215   Dominic Hibberd, "Monro, Harold Edward (1879–1932)," *Oxford Dictionary of National Biography*, Oxford University Press, 2004, www.oxforddnb.com/view/article/35071, retrieved November 24, 2014.

216   See *The Letters of Sylvia Beach*, April 18, 1919.

217   *A Moveable Feast*, UK: Penguin, 1966, p. 30.

218   http://poetryproject.org/ Retrieved November 24, 2014. See also http://poetryproject.org/history/insane-podium/

Index